Lecture Notes in Business Information Processing 568

LNBIP reports state-of-the-art results in areas related to business information systems and industrial application software development – timely, at a high level, and in both printed and electronic form.

The type of material published includes

- Proceedings (published in time for the respective event)
- Postproceedings (consisting of thoroughly revised and/or extended final papers)
- Other edited monographs (such as, for example, project reports or invited volumes)
- Tutorials (coherently integrated collections of lectures given at advanced courses, seminars, schools, etc.)
- Award-winning or exceptional theses

LNBIP is abstracted/indexed in DBLP, EI and Scopus. LNBIP volumes are also submitted for the inclusion in ISI Proceedings.

Krzysztof Węcel
Editor

Business Information Systems Workshops

BIS 2025 International Workshops
Poznań, Poland, June 25–27, 2025
Revised Selected Papers

Springer

Editor
Krzysztof Węcel
Poznań University of Economics and Business
Poznań, Poland

ISSN 1865-1348 ISSN 1865-1356 (electronic)
Lecture Notes in Business Information Processing
ISBN 978-3-032-11650-5 ISBN 978-3-032-11651-2 (eBook)
https://doi.org/10.1007/978-3-032-11651-2

This Springer imprint is published by the registered company Springer Nature Switzerland AG
The registered company address is: Gewerbestrasse 11, 6330 Cham, Switzerland

Preface

In 2025, we gathered in Poznań for the 25th edition of the International Conference on Business Information Systems (BIS). As in previous years, the conference program was enriched with workshops, designed to provide an opportunity to explore topics beyond those outlined in the main call for papers. Workshop organizers were free to choose their own topics provided they were still highly relevant to business information systems research. This year the main theme of the conference was "AI-driven business transformation: challenges and opportunities". Although each workshop had its own focus and autonomy, all of them also were moving towards artificial intelligence, an important trend in business.

Two workshops were held this year: the well-established Workshop on Applications of Knowledge-Based Technologies in Business (AKTB), which had its 13th edition, and the Workshop on Scientific Challenges & Business Opportunities in Sustainable Environmental Management (SciBO-SEM). AKTB focused on knowledge-based business information systems, while the newly established SciBO-SEM addressed the topic of sustainability. At the same time, contributions to both workshops also touched upon the role of AI, thereby strengthening the link with the main conference theme.

The workshops gave authors the opportunity to present their results and ideas to a well-focused audience, and the discussions provided them with valuable perspectives for further research.

Both workshops selected single-blind review type, where each paper had three assigned reviewers. In total, 25 submissions were received for the workshops. From these, 10 papers were selected by the workshop chairs, yielding an acceptance rate of 40%. Based on the feedback received in review and during the BIS conference, the authors were able to revise and extend their papers for this publication.

We would like to express our gratitude to everyone who contributed to the success of the BIS 2025 workshops. In particular, we thank the workshop chairs, members of the Program Committees, the authors of submitted papers, and all participants. We cordially invite you to visit the BIS website at https://bisconf.org/ and to join us at future BIS conferences.

June 2025 Krzysztof Węcel

BIS 2025 Conference Organization

Program Committee Chair

Węcel, Krzysztof	Poznań University of Economics and Business, Poland

Organizing Committee

Lewańska, Elżbieta	Poznań University of Economics and Business, Poland
Lewoniewski, Włodzimierz	Poznań University of Economics and Business, Poland
Stróżyna, Milena	Poznań University of Economics and Business, Poland

AKTB 2025 – 13th Workshop on Applications of Knowledge-Based Technologies in Business

Workshop Chairs

Kriksciuniene, Dalia	Vilnius University, Lithuania
Sakalauskas, Virgilijus	Vilnius University, Lithuania

Program Committee

Baltrusaitis, Paulius	Kauno Kolegija, Lithuania
Bassa, Lia	Foundation for Information Society, Hungary
Kriksciuniene, Dalia	Vilnius University, Lithuania
Lewandowski, Roman	University of Social Sciences, Poland
Lopata, Audrius	Kaunas University of Technology, Lithuania
Luksaite, Dale	Kauno Kolegija, Lithuania
Masteika, Saulius	Vilnius University, Lithuania
Papreckiene, Laima	Kaunas University of Technology, Lithuania
Patalas-Maliszewska, Justyna	University of Zielona Góra, Poland
Pitner, Tomas	Masaryk University, Czech Republic

Romeika, Giedrius	Vilnius University, Lithuania
Romero, José Raúl	University of Córdoba, Spain
Sakalauskas, Virgilijus	Vilnius University, Lithuania

SciBO-SEM – Workshop on Scientific Challenges and Business Opportunities in Sustainable Environmental Management

Workshop Chairs

Mocanu, Mariana	University POLITEHNICA of Bucharest, Romania
Predescu, Alexandru	University POLITEHNICA of Bucharest, Romania

Program Committee

Apostol, Elena-Simona	University POLITEHNICA of Bucharest, Romania
Dobre, Ciprian	University POLITEHNICA of Bucharest, Romania
Ganiyusufoğlu, Ali	University POLITEHNICA of Bucharest, Romania
Hangan, Anca	Technical University of Cluj-Napoca, Romania
Iancu, Bogdan	University POLITEHNICA of Bucharest, Romania
Lemnaru, Camelia	Technical University of Cluj-Napoca, Romania
Mocanu, Mariana	University POLITEHNICA of Bucharest, Romania
Muste, Marian	University of Iowa, USA
Negru, Catalin	University POLITEHNICA of Bucharest, Romania
Pop, Florin	University POLITEHNICA of Bucharest, Romania
Popeanga, Daniel Calin	University POLITEHNICA of Bucharest, Romania
Popescu, Nirvana	University POLITEHNICA of Bucharest, Romania
Predescu, Alexandru	University POLITEHNICA of Bucharest, Romania
Truică, Ciprian-Octavian	University POLITEHNICA of Bucharest, Romania

Contents

AKTB 2025 – 13th Workshop on Applications of Knowledge-Based Technologies in Business

Segmentation for Optimizing Long-Lifecycle Processes in Object-Centric Process Mining

Alessandro Berti[1(✉)], Dina Kretzschmann[1], and Wil M.P. van der Aalst[1,2]

[1] Process and Data Science (PADS), RWTH Aachen University, Aachen, Germany
{a.berti,dina.kretzschmann,wvdaalst}@pads.rwth-aachen.de
[2] Celonis, Munich, Germany

Abstract. Object-centric process mining enables the analysis of complex business processes involving multiple interacting objects, such as in inventory management or e-business workflows. However, long object lifecycles often result in convoluted event logs, obscuring actionable insights and challenging process mining techniques. This paper introduces a segmentation framework that decomposes object-centric event logs into focused, analytically tractable units called segments. We propose segmentation strategies based on object relationships, event types, and temporal intervals, and integrate them with machine learning techniques for anomaly detection and correlation analysis. Implemented in the OC-PM tool, our approach empowers users to uncover localized patterns and optimize process execution. A case study on inventory management demonstrates how segmentation reveals insights into understock and overstock issues, enhancing decision-making in data-intensive domains.

Keywords: Object-Centric Event Logs · Segmentation Strategies · Business Process Optimization · Inventory Management

1 Introduction

Business processes in domains like finance, e-business, and healthcare increasingly involve multiple interacting entities (orders, items, customers, or patients) generating complex event logs that defy traditional process mining's single-case paradigm [14]. Object-centric process mining (OCPM) addresses this by modeling events linked to multiple objects, offering a richer view of real-world workflows such as Purchase-to-Pay (P2P) and Order-to-Cash (O2C). Yet, when objects have long lifecycles spanning numerous events, the resulting data complexity overwhelms standard techniques, obscuring insights critical for optimization [5]. For example, in inventory management, a material might interact with thousands of purchase orders over years, involving events like "Create Purchase Order Item" and "Goods Receipt". A single material's lifecycle could span hundreds of such events, with interleaved stock adjustments (e.g., "Goods Issue" for

K. Wącel (Ed.): BIS 2025 Workshops, LNBIP 568, pp. 3–15, 2026.
https://doi.org/10.1007/978-3-032-11651-2_1

sales), making it nearly impossible to isolate patterns like order delays or stock depletion risks using traditional methods.

To tackle this challenge, we propose a segmentation framework for OCPM, decomposing event logs into manageable units called segments. Unlike traditional flattening approaches, our method defines segments based on object relationships, event types, or temporal intervals. Implemented in the OC-PM tool, this approach enables focused control-flow analysis, anomaly detection, and correlation discovery, transforming raw data into actionable business insights. In the inventory example, segmentation can isolate a material's interactions with a specific purchase order, revealing how order delays contribute to understock situations, thus optimizing resource allocation.

This paper addresses three questions: (1) How can segmentation strategies effectively partition object-centric event logs? (2) How do these segments enhance process optimization through AI analytics? (3) What practical benefits emerge in real-world settings like inventory management? Our contributions include a conceptual framework, an AI-integrated OC-PM extension, and a case study showcasing process improvements.

2 Related Work

This section situates our segmentation framework within the broader landscape of process mining, focusing on object-centric approaches, UI log mining, and computational intelligence applications. We highlight how our work complements and extends existing methodologies, particularly in optimizing complex business processes.

Object-Centric Process Mining: OCPM emerged to address limitations of traditional case-centric mining by modeling events linked to multiple objects [14]. In [15], the discovery of object-centric Petri nets from event logs is proposed, capturing interactions across object types like orders and items. However, such models often become complex when objects exhibit long lifecycles, prompting methods to simplify analysis. In [16], silent objects enhance Petri net precision by accounting for unobserved influences, while [11] introduces a temporal object type model (TOTeM) to capture object-type-level relations (e.g., order-to-invoice precedence). Similarly, [13] proposes object-centric directly-follows graphs (DFGs) for understanding object-centric behavior, and [10] offers granularity adjustments (e.g., drill-down) to focus analysis. Unlike these holistic approaches, our segmentation framework partition logs into focused units, enabling localized insights without requiring new modeling formalisms. By integrating machine learning, we extend OCPM's analytical flexibility, aligning with business optimization goals.

UI Log Mining and Task Segmentation: Process mining on user interface (UI) logs, or task mining, tackles unstructured event streams from user interactions, often for robotic process automation (RPA). In [8], routines are discovered from UI sequences, while [3] employs trace alignment to segment logs into task traces. Similarly, [2] develops an interactive segmentation tool to handle interleaved actions and noise. These methods share our goal of partitioning complex data but focus on sequential user tasks rather than concurrent object interactions. Our approach adapts segmentation to OCPM's multi-object context, managing concurrency, revealing process dynamics, and offering a novel lens for business process analysis beyond RPA.

Computational Intelligence in Process Mining: Computational intelligence enhances process mining by extracting actionable insights from event data. In [9], the IODDA algorithm mines decision rules from object-centric logs, linking object attributes to control-flow decisions. In [1], multivariate anomaly detection identifies deviations in object-centric data, while [4] extracts numerical features for machine learning. Our framework builds on these by embedding AI within segmentation, using techniques like anomaly detection and correlation analysis on segmented logs. This synergy amplifies OCPM's optimization potential, distinguishing our work from global modeling or decision-focused methods.

Positioning and Contribution: Prior OCPM techniques prioritize comprehensive models [11,15], risking complexity, or adjust granularity post-discovery [10]. UI log mining segments sequential data for automation [2], not multi-object processes. Computational intelligence methods enhance analysis but rarely partition event logs [9]. Our segmentation bridges these gaps, offering a preprocessing lens that simplifies OCPM while leveraging machine learning for optimization. Applied to inventory management, it uncovers localized patterns (e.g., stock correlations), advancing smart business modeling for domains like e-business and finance.

3 Background

This section presents the minimal notations for our segmentation framework in OCPM, emphasizing temporal event data for analyzing complex business processes. An *object-centric event log* records events tied to multiple objects, moving beyond traditional single-case mining [14]. Formally, it is a tuple $L = (E, O, T_E, T_O, \mathit{evtype}, \mathit{objtype}, \mathit{rel}, \mathit{time})$, where:

- E is a set of events (e.g., "Create Purchase Order Item");
- O is a set of objects (e.g., a material or purchase order);
- T_E is a set of event types;
- T_O is a set of object types (e.g., "Material", "Purchase Order");
- $\mathit{evtype} : E \rightarrow T_E$ maps each event to its event type;
- $\mathit{objtype} : O \rightarrow T_O$ assigns each object to its object type;
- $\mathit{rel} : E \rightarrow \mathcal{P}(O)$ relates each event to a set of objects;
- $\mathit{time} : E \rightarrow \mathbb{R}^+$ assigns each event a timestamp, a positive real number representing its occurrence time.

For instance, in an inventory log, an event $e \in E$, such as event `e4` ("Goods Receipt") in Table 1, relates to a material $M1$ ($\mathit{objtype}(M1) =$ "Material") and

Table 1. Example object-centric event log, having *Material* as the lead object type.

Ev.ID	Event Activity	Material	PO (Item)
e1	Create Purchase Order Item	M1	PO1
e2	Goods Issue	M1	
e3	Goods Issue	M1	
e4	Goods Receipt	M1	PO1
e5	Goods Issue	M1	
e6	Goods Issue	M1	
e7	Create Purchase Order Item	M1	PO2
e8	Goods Issue	M1	
e9	Goods Issue	M1	
e10	Goods Issue	M1	
e11	Create Purchase Order Item	M1	PO3
e12	Goods Issue	M1	
e13	Goods Receipt	M1	PO3
e14	Delete Purchase Order Item	M1	PO2
e15	Goods Issue	M1	

Table 2. Numeric features for the object-centric event log, including *Material* and *Purchase Order (Item)* objects.

Object Type	Object	# of CPO Item	# of GI	# of GR	# of DPOI	# of Mat. Interactions	# of PO Interactions
Material	M1	3	9	2	1	-	3
Purchase Order	PO1	1	-	1	-	1	-
Purchase Order	PO2	1	-	-	1	1	-
Purchase Order	PO3	1	-	1	-	1	-

a purchase order item $PO1$ ($objtype(PO1)$ = "Purchase Order (Item)"), with $rel(e4) = \{M1, PO1\}$. This aligns with the OCEL standard [7], supporting object-centric, time-ordered analysis. Table 1 illustrates such an event log, showing events like "Create Purchase Order Item" and "Goods Issue" tied to a material and purchase orders. Additionally, Table 2 presents numerical features extracted from this log, such as event counts and object interactions, enabling machine learning applications.

Objects in O have lifecycles over events in $\{e \in E \mid o \in rel(e)\}$, ordered by *time*, often spanning long periods in practice (e.g., materials in inventory). We introduce *segmentation* to partition L into manageable units. A *segment* is a subset $S \subseteq E \times O$ where $(e, o) \in S \implies o \in \text{rel}(e)$, capturing a focused log portion (e.g., events for one purchase order) as a bipartite representation of a sub-log. We store segments as pairs (e, o), so an event e may appear multiple times, once per object it involves. A segmentation strategy $Seg : L \rightarrow \mathcal{P}(\mathcal{P}(E \times O))$ partitions L into a collection $C = \{S_1, S_2, \ldots, S_n\}$, where each segment $S_i \subseteq E \times O$ satisfies $(e, o) \in S_i \Rightarrow o \in rel(e)$.

Key to our approach is the *lead object type*, a type $t_L \in T_O$ (e.g., "Material") with a one-to-many relationship to other types. Formally, each object o_c of a *child object type* $t_C \in T_O$ (e.g., "Purchase Order") relates to exactly one o_L with $objtype(o_L) = t_L$, while o_L may link to multiple o_c. This guides temporal segmentation (e.g., segments per purchase order tied to a material). Events and objects may have *attributes* (e.g., quantities), supporting AI-driven feature extraction [4].

Object-Based Feature Extraction: To enable AI-driven analysis, we transform an object-centric event log $L = (E, O, T_E, T_O, evtype, objtype, rel, time)$ into an *object-based feature table*, where each row corresponds to an object $o \in O$.

Columns represent numerical features derived from the log, capturing object behavior for machine learning tasks like anomaly detection [4].

For an object o, features are computed from its lifecycle $\{e \in E \mid o \in rel(e)\}$. Simple features include:

- *Event counts*: Number of events of a type $t_E \in T_E$ involving o (e.g., count of "Goods Receipt" events for a material).
- *Temporal spans*: Time difference between the earliest and latest events, $\max(\{time(e) \mid o \in rel(e)\}) - \min(\{time(e) \mid o \in rel(e)\})$.
- *Interactions*: Count of distinct objects $o' \in O$ (where $o' \neq o$) sharing events with o, i.e., $|\{o' \mid \exists e : \{o, o'\} \subseteq rel(e)\}|$.

For example, a material $M1$ has 2 "Goods Receipt" events, a lifecycle span from its earliest to latest events, and interactions with 3 purchase order items ($PO1$, $PO2$, $PO3$), as shown in Table 2. Attributes (e.g., quantities) can also be aggregated (e.g., total quantity received). This table, easily constructed via queries on L, supports advanced analytics by converting event sequences into numerical vectors.

4 Approach

Complex object lifecycles in OCPM create significant challenges when trying to extract actionable insights from event logs. To overcome this complexity, we propose segmenting event logs into smaller, more focused subsets. These segments target specific relationships between objects, key event types, or critical time intervals, enabling a more intuitive and effective analysis of processes.

4.1 Segmentation Strategies and Visualization

We propose three main segmentation strategies, each designed to simplify the analysis by focusing on distinct aspects of the event logs:

- **Lead-Child Segmentation:** This strategy focuses on one main object type (the *lead object*) and segments the log according to its relationships with secondary object types (*child objects*). For example, in an inventory scenario, segments can isolate activities related to a specific material and individual purchase orders linked to it. This approach helps clearly identify events correlated to specific orders, making it easier to pinpoint delays or anomalies.
- **Event-Type-Based Segmentation:** Here, segments are created based on specific key events. For instance:
  - *Segments starting from a specific event type:* Events occurring after each instance of a key event (like a "Goods Receipt") until the next occurrence are grouped. This is particularly useful for tracking what happens immediately following critical activities.
  - *Segments ending at a specific event type:* Events leading up to and including a key event are grouped. For example, analyzing activities before each "Goods Receipt" can highlight what contributes to delays.

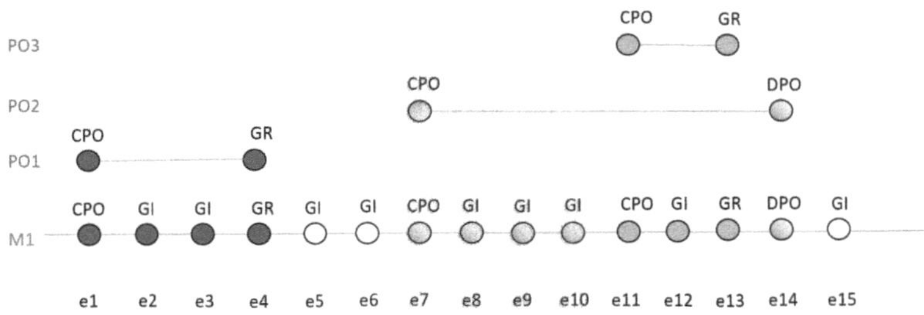

(a) Segments corresponding to the child objects of type purchase order.

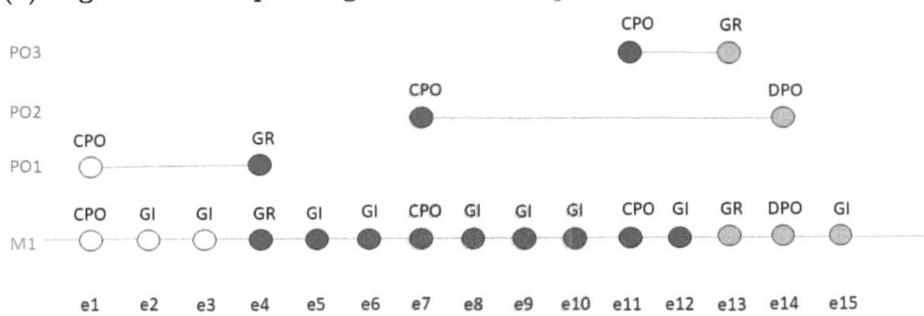

(b) Segments from the event type "Goods Receipt".

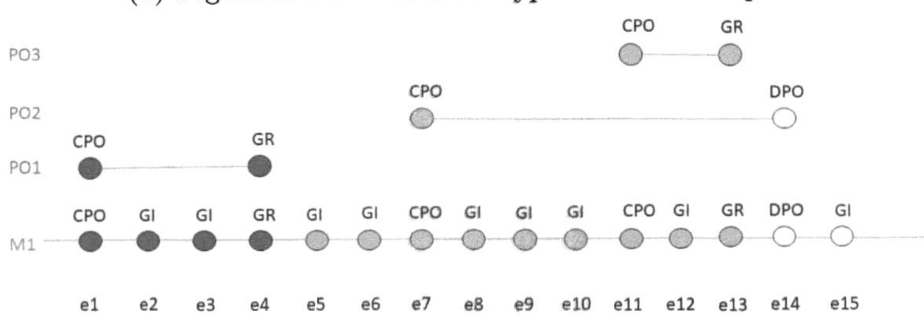

(c) Segments to the event type "Goods Receipt".

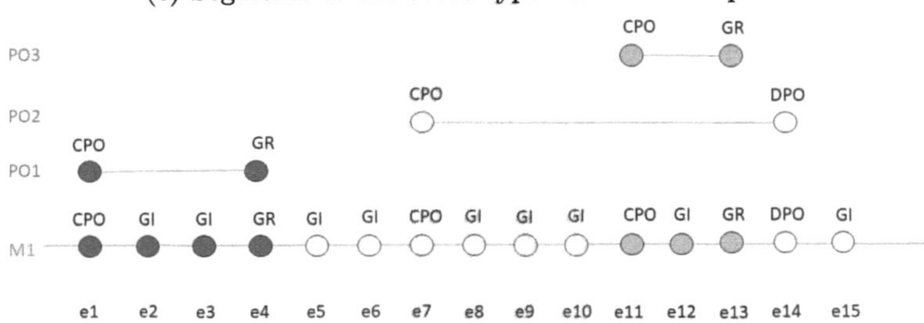

(d) Segments between the event types "Create Purchase Order Item" and "Goods Receipt".

Fig. 1. Proposed segmentation strategies applied in an inventory management context.

- **Temporal Interval-Based Segmentation:** Segments are defined by intervals between two specific event types, capturing complete process phases. For example, considering intervals between "Create Purchase Order Item" and

Table 3. Different segmentation strategies applicable to inventory management. Each segmentation is motivated by different analytical needs.

N.	Type	Lead Object Type	Child Object Type	Source Event Type	Target Event Type	Motivation
1)	Between	Material		Create Purchase Order Item	Goods Receipt	Understanding when the orders are placed too late by discovering understock in the given segments.
2)	Between	Material		Create Purchase Order Suggestion Item	Create Purchase Order Item	Understanding user delays in the order placement phase and alternative reasons for the placement of the purchase orders.
3)	Lead+Child	Material	Purchase Order			Understanding unexpected splits of the receipt of the goods for a given purchase order, resulting potentially in understock situations.
4)	Lead+Child	Material	Sales Order			Identifying orders connected with several goods issues (periodic contracts). Understanding unexpected splits of the goods issue with regards to the initial requested quantity.
5)	To	Material			Create Purchase Order Item	Understanding the reasons leading to triggering a purchase order (such as suggestion from the predictive system, response to sales orders).
6)	From	Material		Goods Receipt		Identifying goods receipts resulting in an initial overstock after the receipt. Observing patterns leading to understock.
7)	To	Material			Goods Receipt	Understanding the correlation between stock status and the number of goods issues.
8)	Between	Supplier		Create Purchase Order Item	Goods Receipt	Assessing the predictability of single suppliers in the provision of the goods.
9)	Between	Customer		Create Sales Order Item	Goods Issue	Assessing customer satisfaction based on prompt responses to sales orders.

"Goods Receipt" makes it easier to analyze the efficiency and timeliness of each procurement cycle.

Figure 1 visually demonstrates these strategies using simplified event names (e.g., "CPO" for "Create Purchase Order Item", "GR" for "Goods Receipt"). Each subfigure clarifies how different strategies segment the log into clearly defined subsets, facilitating easier and more meaningful analyses.

4.2 Improved Activity Sequence Analysis

Segmentation significantly simplifies the analysis of activity sequences by clearly separating relevant activities:

- Without segmentation, event sequences are complex, mixing multiple purchase orders and unrelated events, leading to confusing process flows.
- Applying segmentation, such as the lead-child approach, isolates event sequences tied specifically to individual orders. This reveals simpler, clearer flows—such as a straightforward progression from order creation, through goods issuance, to receipt—making patterns like stock depletion immediately evident.

Such clear sequences enable businesses to identify and directly address specific issues, like reorder delays or inventory shortages, enhancing operational efficiency.

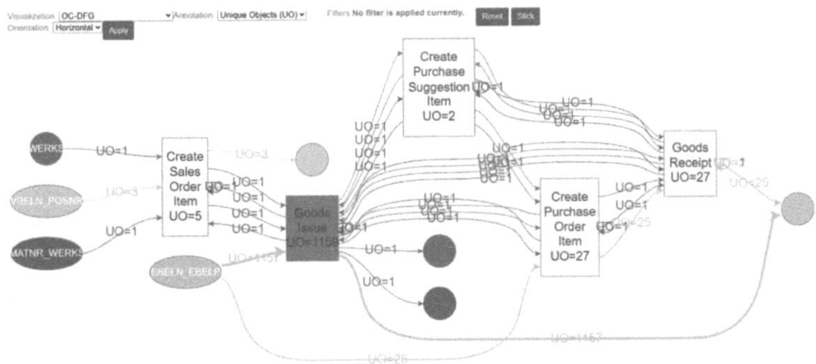

(a) Overall object-centric DFG (as shown by the OC-PM tool) computed before segmentation.

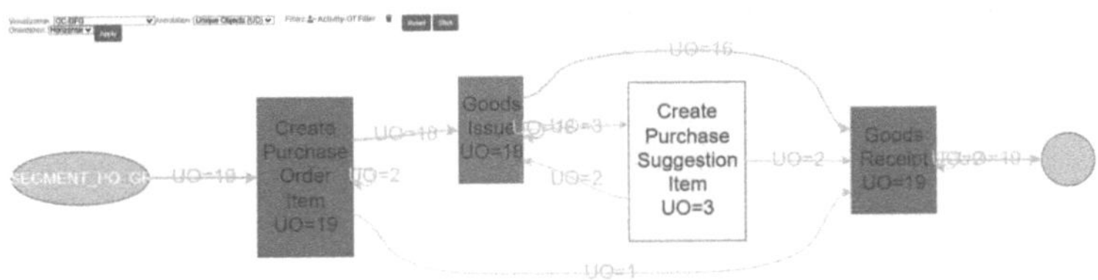

(b) Object-centric DFG (as shown by the OC-PM tool) filtered on the segments object type.

Fig. 2. Combined view of object-centric DFGs before and after segmentation.

Figures 2a and 2b illustrate this transformation. Figure 2a shows the object-centric directly-follows graph (DFG) of the complete event log before segmentation, where numerous overlapping relationships and activities obscure meaningful patterns. In contrast, Fig. 2b shows the DFG after applying segmentation based on object interactions. The resulting structure is significantly more interpretable, emphasizing localized behaviors and process fragments relevant to specific object instances, which enhances the clarity and accuracy of downstream analyses.

4.3 Enhanced Machine Learning Insights

Segmentation also improves the clarity and effectiveness of machine learning analyses:

- Without segmentation, features used for machine learning - like event counts or lifecycle durations - combine unrelated events, resulting in noisy and less insightful analyses.
- With segmentation, each segment provides more meaningful and context-specific features. For example, features computed within a procurement cycle between order creation and receipt clearly indicate stock usage patterns and inventory risks.

Segmented data leads to stronger correlations and more accurate anomaly detection. Businesses can thus precisely target optimization strategies, such as adjusting reorder points or expediting deliveries during identified risk periods.

5 Implementation

To facilitate the practical application of our segmentation framework, we integrated the proposed strategies into the OC-PM tool, a web-based platform designed specifically for object-centric process mining (available at https://www.ocpm.info/). The OC-PM tool supports object-centric event logs in the OCEL 2.0 format and provides functionalities for filtering, analyzing, and visualizing process data.

We enhanced OC-PM by adding a segmentation module accessible through the existing interface, allowing users to easily apply the segmentation strategies outlined earlier. The module provides three straightforward segmentation options (Fig. 3):

- **Lead-Child Segmentation:** Users choose a primary object type (e.g., "Material") and a related secondary type (e.g., "Purchase Order"). The tool automatically segments the log into subsets corresponding to each unique pair, such as individual materials and an associated purchase order.
- **Event-Type-Based Segmentation:** Users select a particular event type (e.g., "Goods Receipt") and decide whether to segment events occurring before or after each occurrence of this event type. This helps users focus on activities immediately surrounding key business events.
- **Temporal Interval-Based Segmentation:** Users define segments based on the intervals between two specific event types (e.g., from "Create Purchase Order Item" to "Goods Receipt"). This clearly isolates complete phases of the process, such as procurement cycles.

Once segments are generated, OC-PM adds them as new "Segment" objects within the log, allowing users to apply further analyses or filtering directly within the tool.

The segmentation module significantly enhances OC-PM's analysis capabilities. Users can visualize simplified and focused process flows for each segment, greatly improving the readability of complex event logs. Additionally, users can query segmented logs using an intuitive interface to explore specific subsets of interest, aggregate data, or investigate specific issues such as procurement delays or stock depletion.

Moreover, OC-PM provides integrated support for machine learning analyses [4,12]. It automatically computes relevant features from each segment, such as event counts or durations, enabling correlation analyses and anomaly detection directly within segmented logs. This integration allows users to easily identify and act upon patterns or anomalies that might be hidden in a non-segmented view.

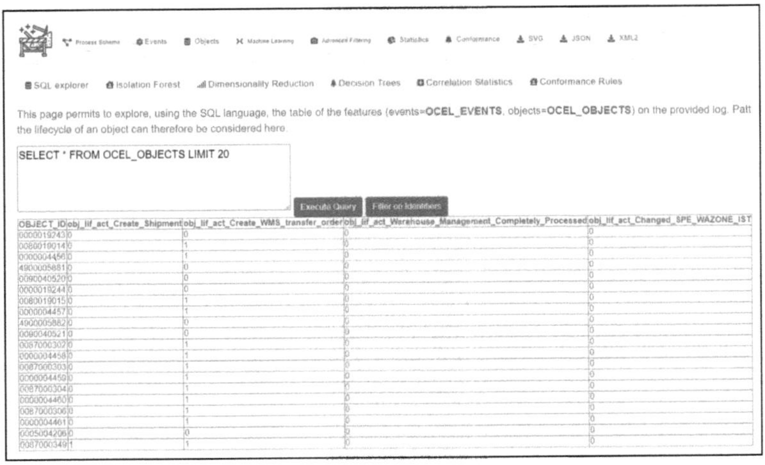

(a) SQL explorer of the numerical features (as shown by the OC-PM tool), allowing for filtering/aggregation.

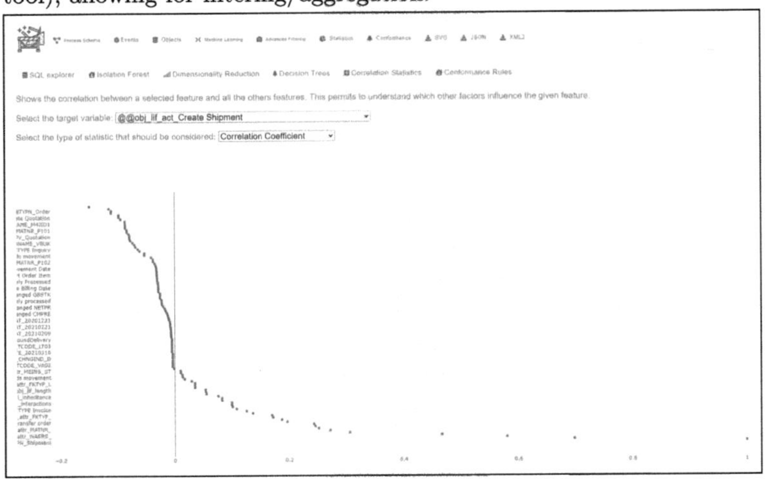

(b) Correlation statistics between the different features.

Fig. 3. Some ML features offered in the OC-PM tool.

6 Case Study

We evaluated the effectiveness of our segmentation approach through a case study involving inventory management at a retail company. The company faced challenges with maintaining optimal stock levels, frequently experiencing under-stock and overstock issues. Their goal was to improve inventory efficiency by gaining clearer insights into the underlying causes of these issues.

The case study utilized a real-world object-centric event log that combined processes from purchasing (Purchase-to-Pay) and sales (Order-to-Cash). The event log includes various types of objects, such as materials, suppliers, customers, and purchase orders, along with event attributes like quantities and stock levels. A simplified example of the data is provided in Table 4, where specific thresholds for safety stock (SS) and overstock (OS) are defined.

Table 4. Simplified extract of the object-centric event log considered in the case study. We assume that for the material $M001$, $SS = 91$ and $OS = 150$. The event log is available at https://zenodo.org/records/13347782.

Transformed Event Type	Material	Supplier	Customer	PO Item	Quantity	Stock Before	Stock After
Goods Issue	M001		C001		2	100	98
Goods Issue	M001		C002		3	98	95
Create Purchase Suggestion Item	M001	S001			100	95	95
Create Purchase Order Item	M001	S001		PO1	100	95	95
Goods Issue	M001		C003		5	95	90
Goods Receipt	M001	S001		PO1	50	90	140
Goods Receipt	M001	S001		PO1	50	140	190
Goods Issue	M001		C001		10	190	180

Initially, analyzing the complete, unsegmented event log proved challenging due to its complexity and the overlapping lifecycles of multiple purchase orders and sales events. The resulting visualizations and analyses lacked clarity, making it difficult to pinpoint precise issues affecting inventory levels.

We applied several segmentation strategies from the OC-PM tool to address this complexity:

- **Lead-Child Segmentation (Material-Purchase Order):** By segmenting events related to each specific material-purchase order pair, we isolated the activities correlated to individual orders. This segmentation clarified the flow of each order cycle, clearly identifying events such as goods issues and receipts for each order.
- **Temporal Interval-Based Segmentation (from order creation to goods receipt):** This approach focused specifically on procurement phases. It clearly highlighted procurement timelines and helped identify periods where delays caused stock to fall below safety thresholds or exceed overstock levels.

Applying these segmentations yielded significant clarity improvements, revealing key insights for inventory management. Segmentation clearly identified instances where goods were ordered prematurely or in excessive quantities, leading to significant overstock situations after receipt, while also isolating procurement cycles to detect specific cases where delayed orders caused stock to fall below safe thresholds, thus highlighting critical reordering issues. Moreover, segmented data enhanced machine learning analyses, clarifying correlations between goods issues and stock levels with strong negative correlations in specific procurement cycles that were previously obscured in the complete dataset, and enabled precise identification of anomalous stock movements, such as unusually large goods issues or unexpectedly high stock levels after receipts, which are crucial for accurate inventory management.

Overall, segmentation significantly improved the company's ability to identify and understand inventory management issues. These insights led directly to actionable recommendations, such as adjusting reorder points, optimizing order quantities, and managing stock more proactively, ultimately enhancing operational efficiency and reducing inventory-related costs.

7 Discussion and Conclusions

This paper introduced a segmentation framework for object-centric process mining (OCPM) to tackle the complexity of long and intricate object lifecycles in event logs. By partitioning logs based on object relationships, event types, and temporal intervals, our approach enhances the clarity and interpretability of process data, addressing challenges that traditional methods struggle to overcome. The integration of this framework into the OC-PM tool, as demonstrated in our inventory management case study, revealed actionable insights—such as overstock and understock patterns and anomalous demand behaviors—that were obscured in unsegmented analyses. These findings directly informed operational improvements, including optimized reorder points and better purchase order timing, driving efficiency and cost reduction in inventory processes.

Despite these advancements, our approach has limitations. First, the effectiveness of segmentation relies on user expertise in selecting appropriate strategies (e.g., choosing relevant object types or event intervals), as outlined in Table 3. Inappropriate choices may lead to incomplete or misleading insights. Second, the framework assumes well-structured, high-quality event logs; noisy or incomplete data, common in real-world settings, can degrade segment quality and subsequent analyses. Third, computational costs may increase for very large logs, as segmenting and analyzing numerous subsets demands significant resources. These constraints highlight the need for careful application and potential preprocessing to ensure data quality.

Our segmentation framework lays a robust foundation for future work in OCPM and related fields. By breaking complex logs into focused, analyzable units, it enables researchers and practitioners to uncover localized patterns and correlations, as seen in our case study's improved anomaly detection and stock correlation insights. Future studies can exploit this approach by integrating automated segmentation strategy selection, leveraging AI techniques like large language models to recommend optimal partitions based on log characteristics [6]. Additionally, combining segmentation with predictive analytics could forecast process bottlenecks or resource needs, enhancing proactive decision-making.

References

1. Abb, L., Rehse, J.: Multivariate anomaly detection in object-centric event data. In: BPM Conference, pp. 20–36. Springer (2024)

2. Agostinelli, S., Leotta, F., Marrella, A.: Interactive segmentation of user interface logs. In: ICSOC Conference, pp. 65–80. Springer (2021)
3. Agostinelli, S., Marrella, A., Mecella, M.: Automated segmentation of user interface logs. In: Robotic Process Automation, pp. 201–222. De Gruyter Oldenbourg (2021)
4. Berti, A., Herforth, J., Qafari, M., van der Aalst, W.: Graph-based feature extraction on object-centric event logs. Int. J. Data Sci. Anal. **18**(2), 139–155 (2024)
5. Berti, A., Jessen, U., Park, G., Rafiei, M., van der Aalst, W.: Analyzing interconnected processes: using object-centric process mining to analyze procurement processes. Int. J. Data Sci. Anal. 1–23 (2023)
6. Berti, A., Jessen, U., van der Aalst, W., Dirk Fahland: Explainable Object-Centric Anomaly Detection: the Role of Domain Knowledge. In: BPM-D Forum, pp. 162–168. CEUR-WS.org (2024)
7. Berti, A., et alet al.: Ocel (object-centric event log) 2.0 specification. arXiv:2403.01975 (2024)
8. Bosco, A., Augusto, A., Dumas, M., La Rosa, M., Fortino, G.: Discovering automatable routines from user interaction logs. In: BPM Forum, pp. 144–162. Springer (2019)
9. Goossens, A., De Smedt, J., Vanthienen, J.: Extracting process-aware decision models from object-centric process data. Inf. Sci. **682**, 121263 (2024)
10. Khayatbashi, S., Miri, N., Jalali, A.: Advancing object-centric process mining with multi-dimensional data operations. arXiv:2412.00393 (2024)
11. Liss, L., Adams, J., van der Aalst, W.: Totem: Temporal object type model for object-centric process mining. In: BPM Conference, pp. 107–123. Springer (2024)
12. Liu, F., Ting, K., Zhou, Z.: Isolation forest. In: ICDM Conference, pp. 413–422. IEEE (2008)
13. Park, G., Adams, J., van der Aalst, W.: Conformance checking and performance analysis using object-centric directly-follows graphs. In: BPM Conference, pp. 179–196. Springer (2024)
14. van der Aalst, W.: Object-centric process mining: unraveling the fabric of real processes. Math. **11**(12), 2691 (2023)
15. van der Aalst, W.: Alessandro Berti: Discovering object-centric petri nets. Fundam. Inform. **175**(1–4), 1–40 (2020)
16. van Detten, J., Schumacher, P., Leemans, S.J.: Object Synchronizations and Specializations with Silent Objects in Object-Centric Petri Nets. In: BPM Conference, pp. 57–74. Springer (2024)

Supporting the Mental Health Care with Artificial Intelligence Chatbots

Dominika Smoczyńska and Agata Filipowska(✉)

Department of Information Systems, Poznan University of Economics and Business,
Al. Niepodleglosci 10, 61-875 Poznań, Poland
agata.filipowska@ue.poznan.pl
https://kie.ue.poznan.pl/pl/agata-filipowska/

Abstract. The widespread nature of mental health challenges, combined with the advancement of artificial intelligence and the advent of large language models, inspired the authors to investigate the potential role of AI-driven chatbots in mental health care.

The goal of this research is to review performance of five AI-based chatbots in tasks from the area of the mental health care. These chatbots were implemented based on the guidelines provided by their developers, extended when needed, and evaluated using the carefully designed set of questions.

The paper presents results of this review as well as compares the results with state of the art within the field.

Keywords: mental health · AI chatbots

1 Introduction

An increasing number of people, including children and youth, face mental health issues that hinder emotional regulation and social functioning. The COVID-19 pandemic and the war in Ukraine exacerbated these problems, leading to greater isolation, economic recession, and inflation, sparking uncertainties about the future and a lack of stability [2,26].

Modern stressors like the fast-paced lifestyle, information overload, and social media also impact mental well-being, especially among young people [6,13]. Unfortunately, access to psychological and psychiatric care remains limited worldwide, with rural areas and small towns often lacking proper funding and resources [26]. Stigmatization of mental health continues, and financial barriers aggravate the situation with long waiting times for specialists or high costs for private care.

Despite these challenges, young people increasingly advocate for mental health awareness and well-being, considering it an investment in self-care. We also observe emergence of AI-based solutions. AI-powered chatbots, designed to mimic conversations with therapists, could improve access to psychological

K. Wącel (Ed.): BIS 2025 Workshops, LNBIP 568, pp. 16–27, 2026.
https://doi.org/10.1007/978-3-032-11651-2_2

services by providing immediate support and ensuring user anonymity, reducing fears of stigma. Additionally, these solutions could assist psychotherapists in monitoring patients' conditions through app-generated analyses, enabling more tailored therapy.

The widespread nature of mental health challenges, combined with the advancement of artificial intelligence and the advent of large language models, inspired the authors to investigate the potential role of AI-driven chatbots in mental health care. As part of this exploration, market-available solutions were reviewed, and the feasibility of developing innovative tools leveraging large language models was examined. A comparative analysis was carried out using five implementations built with these sophisticated models.

2 AI Chatbots in the Mental Health Care

2.1 Application Scenarios

Psychological chatbots primarily support doctors and psychotherapists in treating their patients. They provide mental health assistance at any time and place, eliminating the need for appointments or travel to specialists. However, they are not intended to replace professionals. Chatbots can track a patient's mood through conversations and questionnaires, generating periodic reports for therapists to aid therapy planning. They also detect drastic mood changes and alert specialists immediately [8].

Chatbots can also function independently, tracking users' moods and suggesting screening tests for depression, if needed. Many offer mindfulness exercises and stress reduction techniques. Worth to notice is that chatbots reduce healthcare worker burdens by addressing mental health issues early [18]. Moreover, chatbots also contribute to mental health education. Specialists stress however that serious mental disorders require professional intervention and not sole reliance on chatbots [14].

Among potential application of psychological chatbots, the following ones are perceived as key: supporting therapy for specialists and patients, diagnosis, monitoring mental health, providing mental health content. Despite their progress within last years, the full potential of psychological chatbots is still to be experienced.

2.2 Existing Solutions in the Area of the Mental Health Care

The AI chatbot market is currently experiencing significant growth. In 2022, the global market for mental health and therapy chatbots was valued at nearly one billion dollars, but it is estimated to exceed approximately 6.51 billion dollars by 2032, growing at a compound annual growth rate of 21.3% [25]. Figure 1 illustrates the revenue projections for the market through 2032 in billions of dollars.

The most popular chatbots currently supporting mental health are Woebot, Wysa [15] and Youper. They are shortly presented in the following paragraphs,

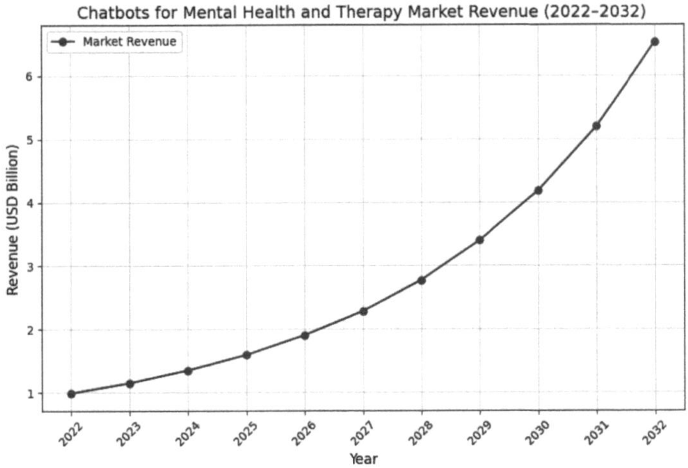

Fig. 1. Revenue projections for the AI therapy chatbots in billions of dollars. Source: own study based on [25].

especially that they provide inspiration and the baseline for solutions subject to experimentation in the second part of this paper.

Woebot, launched in 2017 by Woebot Labs, is an AI-driven chatbot leveraging cognitive-behavioral therapy (CBT) techniques to assist users in managing their mental health, particularly symptoms of depression. Unlike generative chatbots like ChatGPT, Woebot operates based on rules, with conversations crafted by trained authors in collaboration with clinical experts. It uses natural language processing to understand user input and provide appropriate therapeutic responses and activities, such as CBT exercises for anxiety or sleep. Available primarily to U.S. users with access codes through specific healthcare partners, Woebot is used by 1.5 million people. It offers interactive conversations, progress tracking, and personalized challenges, emphasizing empathy and evidence-based guidance [1].

Wysa, developed by Touchkin in 2016, is an AI-powered mental health chatbot using cognitive-behavioral therapy techniques, meditation, yoga, and motivational conversations to support emotional well-being. Similar to Woebot, Wysa focuses on self-help and managing emotions but does not diagnose or treat disorders. Its AI learns from user input to improve responses while maintaining clinical safety through a rule-based engine. Unlike Woebot, Wysa also offers access to human specialists through a premium plan. Awarded "Best App" by Google Play in 2020, Wysa's broader availability gives it a competitive edge [27,28].

Youper, launched in 2016 by psychiatrist Jose Hamilton, combines cognitive-behavioral therapy and positive psychology techniques to help users manage their mental health. The app personalizes its approach by monitoring users' mental states through conversations, creating insights, charts, and summaries that users can share with healthcare professionals to optimize treatment. Unlike Wysa and

Woebot, Youper blends rule-based methods with generative AI, producing flexible, human-like responses. This innovative combination offers research potential but also introduces risks [7,9,22,29].

Table 1 presents a comparison of these three most popular applications enabling conversations with psychotherapeutic chatbots based on cognitive-behavioural therapy techniques. From the authors' perspective, the best solution, primarily due to its availability, is the Wysa app that has also received very high ratings among users on Google Play (rating 4.7, compared to Youper's 4.2).

Table 1. Comparison of the three most popular applications enabling conversations with psychotherapeutic chatbots

	Woebot	Wysa	Youper
Launch	2017	2016	2016
Technology	Rule-based	Rule-based	Combination of a rule-based approach and a generative neural network.
Functions	24/7 conversations with a chatbot using cognitive-behavioral therapy techniques. Therapeutic exercises. A dashboard with analysis and statistics on well-being over the long term.	24/7 conversations with a chatbot using cognitive-behavioral therapy techniques. Therapeutic exercises. Option to schedule a conversation with a specialist.	24/7 conversations with a chatbot using cognitive-behavioral therapy techniques. Long-term mental state monitoring, statistics, and charts. Initial interview on mental health enabling personalization. Option to share data with specialists.
Access	Access can be obtained as an employee of a company partnered with Woebot or by using a healthcare system partnered with Woebot.	Available for free, however there are premium versions with additional therapeutic exercises or possibility to contact a specialist through the app.	Paid application.

Source: own study

2.3 Advantages and Limitations of AI Chatbots Application in the Mental Health Care

Psychological chatbots offer many benefits, such as increased accessibility to psychological services and the ability to provide support during critical moments. Thanks to learning algorithms, they can deliver personalized support and ensure anonymity, which helps combat stigmatization. They also assist professionals by suggesting diagnoses and therapeutic paths and support users after therapy, helping to prevent relapses [5,8,23].

However, using chatbots comes also with limitations. They may provide incorrect or harmful advice, fail to recognize non-verbal signals, and can be biased due to algorithmic limitations. There is a risk of users mistakenly believing that technology can replace a therapist, which may hinder seeking proper treatment. Chatbots also struggle to detect crisis situations, such as suicidal thoughts. Additionally, a significant concern is the lack of data privacy – users' information may be exposed to leaks, cyberattacks, or unethical use by companies [8,18].

The research presented in this paper aims to examine the extent to which AI-based chatbots can enhance existing solutions, such as Wysa or Woebot, which are primarily rule-based. The goal is to evaluate whether AI-driven chatbots can provide a more human-like experience and expand the range of support offered by these applications or similar ones. To achieve this, we analyze the behavior of five different chatbots in predefined scenarios. The details of the experimental setup and the implementation of these chatbots are provided in the next section of the paper.

3 Examining Chatbots to Support the Mental Health Care

3.1 Goal of the Experiment

The goal of the experiment that was carried out in this research project was to present different approaches to implementation of AI-based chatbots supporting mental health that could enrich the set of existing solutions, at the same time providing a required level of users security. To achieve this goal, five chatbots were examined and compared. These chatbots togehter with their implementation will be described in the following sections.

First two use neural networks and aim to select a response from the provided dataset that is most likely to meet the user's needs. Third chatbot also utilizes a neural network model, however, its creator's goal was to develop a program capable of generating new responses based on data from the available knowledge base. The last two, the most advanced chatbots, employ the large language models, and were developed by the leaders in the field (Meta and OpenAI).

The chatbots are compared, with both their key features summarized and their effectiveness in answering a specific set of questions analysed.

3.2 Datasets Used in the Experiment

To train or enrich knowledge base of chatbots included in the experiment, two different datasets were used (details on how each chatbot was prepared for the needs of the experiment are described in Sect. 3.3). One of the datasets (in JSON format) used to train the selected chatbots was created by combining two datasets: Intents (JSON format) from kaggle.com[1] [19] and a smaller dataset of the same

[1] https://www.kaggle.com/code/jocelyndumlao/chatbot-for-mental-health-conversations/input.

title from gist.github.com[2] [12]. The dataset contains a collection of conversations related to mental health, including basic exchanges, frequently asked questions about mental health, classic therapeutic discussions, and general advice for individuals dealing with anxiety and depression. The dataset may enable training of a chatbot model that emulates a therapist, capable of providing empathetic and supportive responses.

The second dataset used within the research was Mental Health FAQ for Chatbot from kaggle.com[3] [17]. This dataset is in CSV format with three columns: question_ID, questions, and answers, containing 98 rows. The questions column includes potential mental health-related questions, while the answers column provides responses to these questions. The CSV file was used to create a content-generating chatbot as it does not require the tags included in the previously discussed JSON file.

3.3 Implementation of Chatbots Used in the Experiment

As mentioned, five different AI chatbots were used within the performed research. Each of them needed to be configured or re-trained using the datasets collected by the authors. First chatbot, based on PyTorch, was developed by Kevin Liu [11]. The goal was to create a bot promoting awareness and education on mental health. The chatbot draws its knowledge from the previously mentioned Intents dataset. The development of the chatbot consisted of three key steps (that needed to be performed by authors of this work, using provided implementation): transforming conversational intents and definitions into a PyTorch model, creating the chatbot framework for response processing, building a graphical user interface.

Second chatbot, based on Keras Sequential, was presented by Zaid Shaikh [21]. The author aimed to create a chatbot that would improve access to psychological support for individuals facing mental health challenges. The functionality of the chatbot is similar to the one previously discussed, as it also uses the Intents dataset (in JSON file). A user's question is classified into one of the intents, after which the user receives one of the possible responses. The primary difference between the previous chatbot and the current one lies in the library used to build the neural network model. While the previous chatbot utilized PyTorch, Shaik opted for the Keras library, which simplifies the construction, training, and evaluation of models [24]. Another key difference is the lack of a graphical user interface. The chatbot's development, as carried out in this research, can be divided into four main steps: preprocessing natural language using the NLTK library, training the neural network model with Keras, preparing methods to process user responses, and testing.

The third chatbot included in the study was created by Anuradh Pandey, with its source code available on GitHub [16]. Unlike the previously discussed chatbots, this one utilizes the previously described data in the CSV format

---

2 https://gist.github.com/kevin-liu-tech/cca48c49f9d181d31f3dd97013c018dc#file-intents-json.

3 https://www.kaggle.com/datasets/narendrageek/mental-health-faq-for-chatbot.

and is a generative chatbot. Instead of directly returning pre-written responses from the dataset, it aims to generate new responses inspired by the dataset's content. Similarly to other bots described in the study, this chatbot uses natural language processing techniques to analyze text data and emulate patterns of human conversation. The chatbot relies on a seq2seq model employing LSTM for generating text from the training corpus. Its development can be divided into three key steps: text preprocessing using NLP methods, training the LSTM model, and implementing user message processing and response generation.

Fourth chatbot, the chatbot using the Llama2 model was developed by creators of the DataInsightEdge YouTube channel [3], with its source code available on GitHub [4]. The authors aimed to create a healthcare-oriented chatbot capable of responding to user questions about mental health. Unlike other chatbots, this model uses a PDF file—Defining Mental Health and Mental Illness [10] - as its data source (in addition to the previously described files with data). The PDF document explains mental health, mental illnesses, and related issues, such as social stigma. The chatbot's goal is to absorb the knowledge from the PDF document so that it can answer any user inquiries related to its content. The main advantage of this approach is that it does not merely return verbatim responses from the source data, as most JSON-based chatbots do; instead, it generates its own responses.

When comparing various implementations of chatbots designed for mental health support, the use of the model developed by OpenAI could not be overlooked. Oladimeji Samuel undertook the implementation of a chatbot utilising OpenAI model, publishing a tutorial on medium.com[4] [20]. This chatbot uses the previously discussed dataset in the CSV format. Leveraging existing models, the required code is minimal, and the chatbot's development can be divided into two key steps: invoking the model with appropriate parameters and data, and creating a short API to handle user queries.

Table 2 summarizes the details of the chatbot implementations presented within the section. It includes data about the libraries and tools used to develop the chatbot by its original authors, datasets employed for model training, the chatbots' ability to generate new responses beyond the ones provided in the dataset, the presence of a graphical user interface, whether the solution is free, and the time required to generate a response.

It needs to be mentioned that models using the PyTorch and Keras libraries offer valuable insight into the entire process of preparing and operating a neural network model, unlike chatbots leveraging Llama2 and OpenAI models, which function as "black boxes". However, the latter are considered the most effective solutions as they can generate new, interesting responses beyond the content directly provided in the dataset. When comparing these two models, the OpenAI-based model has a significant speed advantage. However, the program using Meta's Llama2 model is entirely free, includes an implemented user interface,

[4] https://medium.com/@oladimejisamuel/building-a-mental-health-chatbot-using-fastapi-langchain-and-openai-1e22d9c6edc1.

and allows the addition of new data simply by uploading a new PDF file with additional information.

Table 2. Comparison of chatbots used in the experiment

	Chatbot based on Pytorch	Chatbot based on Keras	Chatbot generating responses	Chatbot based on Llama2	Chatbot based on OpenAI
Dataset used to enhance knowledge base	Intents (JSON format)	Intents (JSON format)	Q&A (CSV file)	PDF file	Q&A (CSV file)
Libraries	Pytorch – NeuralNet; NLTK	Keras – Sequentional; NLTK	Keras – LSTM, Model; NLTK	Llama2; HuggingFaceEmbeddings; FAISS	LangChain; OpenAI
User interface	Yes, Tkinter library	No	No	Yes, Streamlit library	No
Does it generate new responses?	No	No	After first response, incomplete	Yes	Yes
Is the solution free?	Yes	Yes	Yes	Yes	No
Response time	Immediate	Immediate	Immediate	About a minute	Couple of seconds

Source: own study

3.4 Experiment Overview

After configuration of the chatbots described in the previous subsection, an experiment was carried out using these chatbots. Each of the chatbots was exposed to the following set of questions:

1. a query directly included in the provided dataset,
2. a query containing a keyword from the dataset,
3. a query containing a keyword from the dataset but in a different form,
4. a query with a similar meaning to one in the dataset,
5. a query related to mental health but not included in the dataset.

The specific questions asked were as follows:

1. What's the difference between sadness and depression? This exact query is included in the datasets.
2. I think I have depression. The query is not directly in the dataset, but several questions contain the word depression.

3. I have suicidal thoughts. There is no question in the dataset containing the word suicidal, but there is a question with the word suicide.
4. I cry because of my parents' death. This query was deliberately designed to lack any keywords. However, its intent is similar to that of a query related to the loss of a loved one, which is included in the dataset.
5. I lost passion for living. This query is not included in the dataset.

Before asking questions to the chatbots, a list of answers was developed to compare against the received results. Table 3 presents results of the tests that will be discussed in the next section.

3.5 Results and Discussion

All chatbots except the generative one are capable of providing satisfactory responses to a defined set of questions. The generative model would require additional work to improve its effectiveness.

While evaluating the first two chatbots that returned responses from the JSON file, the authors aimed to receive answers where the intent matched the question, was similar, or simply made logical sense. Of the two, the chatbot using the Keras library performed better. Unfortunately, the generative model did not perform well with any of the questions. The chatbot using OpenAI handled every question exceptionally well. Additionally, when asked about suicidal thoughts, the model responded empathetically, stating it was sorry but unable to help in such a case and advised the user to directly consult a specialist—this is considered a desirable behaviour.

For the chatbot built using the Llama2 model, the authors had to use a different set of questions due to the content of the PDF file being distinct from the other files. The first three questions address topics directly discussed in the PDF, while the last two questions are unrelated to the information in the file.

1. *Define mental health.* Good response, the chatbot answered based on the PDF file.
2. *What about children and mental illness?* Good response, the chatbot answered based on the PDF file.
3. *I think I have depression.* Good response, the chatbot answered based on the PDF file.
4. *I cry because of my parents' death.* Good response.
5. *I lost passion for living.* Poor response, the chatbot did not understand the intent.

Overall, the OpenAI-based chatbot performed the best across all questions, with Llama following its results. This may suggest that a chatbot based on OpenAI could be more suitable for broader applications. However, this is still to be verified in the future research, where the two best chatbots are to be subject to a more extensive testing and evaluation, also from the cost perspective.

Table 3. Comparison of answers returned using chatbots

	Chatbot based on Pytorch	Chatbot based on Keras	Chatbot generating responses	Chatbot based on OpenAI
Query directly included in the provided dataset.	Correct answer	Correct answer	Wrong answer	Correct answer
Query containing a keyword from the dataset.	Correct answer	Correct answer	Wrong answer	Correct answer
Query containing a keyword from the dataset but in a different form.	Wrong answer	Correct answer	Wrong answer	Correct answer
Query with a similar meaning to one in the dataset.	Wrong answer	Wrong answer	Wrong answer	Correct answer
Query related to mental health but not included in the dataset.	Wrong answer (chat informs that it does not understand)	Partially correct answer	Wrong answer	Correct answer

Source: own study

4 Conclusions

This paper presented five implementations of chatbots designed to support users' mental health. The programs differed in the technologies used, their ability to generate new responses, interface implementation, and response time. Two out of five chatbots in the training process utilized an Intents dataset containing a set of intents and conversations related to mental health, two were trained using a CSV file with a set of questions and answers, and another used a PDF file with a scientific article.

Regarding effectiveness, both the chatbot using the Keras library and the one using PyTorch performed well in matching responses from the dataset to user queries. Their main drawback, however, was the inability to generate new responses, overreaching the provided dataset. The chatbot intended to generate new responses using an LSTM neural network failed entirely, as it could not produce answers to any of the given queries during testing.

As expected, the best-performing models were those using large language models. The solution with the Llama2 model stood out for being free, having an implemented user interface, and offering ease in integrating new knowledge. However, the chatbot utilizing the OpenAI model performed slightly better in providing responses to questions asked.

Future work will encompass more complex efficiency tests for the two top-performing chatbots to confirm or refute the initial conclusions regarding the effectiveness of these solutions.

References

1. AIFund. Woebot Health (2024). https://woebothealth.com/ [Access 30 May 2024]
2. Ceglarz, J.: W tej kwestii zgadzamy się wszyscy. Polacy boją się wojny [SONDAŻ] (2024). https://businessinsider.com.pl/wiadomosci/w-tej-kwestii-zgadzamy-sie-wszyscy-polacyboja-sie-wojny-sondaz/bgdg0g7 [Access 19 May 2024]
3. DataInsightEdge. Build Streamlit HealthCare Chatbot with Llama 2 and Langchain on CPU Machine with MEMORY|All OPEN SOURCE (2023). https://www.youtube.com/watch?v=XNmFIkViEBU [Access 13 Apr 2024]
4. DataInsightEdge. LLama2HealthCareChatBot (2023). https://github.com/InsightEdge01/LLama2HealthCareChatBot/tree/master [Access 13 Apr 2024]
5. Farvolden, P.: AI chatbots break down barriers to much-needed mental health treatments (2024). https://www.rgare.com/knowledge-center/article/ai-chatbots-break-downbarriers-to-much-needed-mental-health-treatments [Access 30 May 2024]
6. Folk, J.: Why is mental illness on the rise? (2021). https://www.anxietycentre.com/faq/why-is-mentalillness-on-the-rise/ [Access 19 May 2024]
7. Joseph, S.: What happened to YOUPER and can AI replace therapy? (2022). https://syljoe.medium.com/whathappened-to-youper-and-can-ai-replace-therapy-37c690b0026b [Access 30 May 2024].
8. Khawaja, Z., Bélisle-Pipon, J.C.: Your robot therapist is not your therapist: understanding the role of AI-powered mental health chatbots. Front. Digit. Health (2023)
9. Kidane, M.: AI and behavioral health: what every clinician should know (2024). https://helloalma.com/blog/ai-&-behavioral-health:-what-every-clinician-should-know/ [Access 30 May 2024]
10. Leighton, S., Dogra, N.: Defining mental health and mental illness (2009). https://www.researchgate.net/publication/255657987_Defining_mental_health_and_mental_illness
11. Liu, K.: Building a chatbot for mental health awareness and education (2021). https://chatbotslife.com/building-a-chatbot-for-mental-health-awareness-and-education-262ecd596591 [Access 11 Apr 2024]
12. Liu, K.: intents.json (2021). https://gist.github.com/kevin-liu-ech/cca48c49f9d181d31f3dd97013c018dc#file-intents-json [Access 11 Apr 2024].
13. MacMillan, A.: 4 possible reasons why mental health is getting worse (2023). https://www.health.com/condition/depression/8-million-americans-psychologicaldistress [Access 19 May 2024]
14. Metcalf, M.: The best mental health chatbots in 2024 (2024). https://getmarlee.com/blog/mental-health-chatbot#toc-section-1 [Access 30 May 2024]
15. Mordor Intelligence. Artificial Intelligence (AI)-powered mental health solutions market size and share analysis - growth trends and forecasts (2024 – 2029) (2024). https://www.mordorintelligence.com/industry-reports/ai-powered-mental-health-solutions-market [Access 30 May 2024]
16. Pandey, A.: Chatbot for mental health (2021).https://github.com/pandeyanuradha/Chatbot-for-mental-health [Access 13 Apr 2024]

17. Prasath, N.: Mental health FAQ for chatbot (2020). https://www.kaggle.com/datasets/narendrageek/mentalhealth-faq-for-chatbot [Access 13 Apr 2024]
18. Psychologs. the role of chatbots in mental health services: how does it impact people? (2024). https://www.psychologs.com/the-role-of-chatbots-in-mental-health-services-how-does-it-impact-people/ [Access 30 May 2024]
19. Roe, A.: Chatbot for mental health conversations (2023). https://www.kaggle.com/code/jocelyndumlao/chatbot-for-mental-health-conversations/input [Access 11 April 2024]
20. Samuel, O.: Building a mental health chatbot using FastAPI, Langchain, and OpenAI in python. In: (2023). https://medium.com/@oladimejisamuel/building-a-mental-health-chatbot-usingfastapi-langchain-and-openai-1e22d9c6edc1
21. Shaikh, Z.: Let's build a chatbot for mental health (2021). https://111zack333.medium.com/lets-build-achatbot-for-mental-health-1a270ad3e70 [Access 12 April 2024]
22. Sprintis, R.: Youper App Review 2024: Pros and Cons, Cost, and Who It's Right For (2024). https://www.choosingtherapy.com/youper-app-review/ [Access 30 May 2024]
23. Sweeney, C., et al.: Can chatbots help support a person's mental health? perceptions and views from mental healthcare professionals and experts. In: ACM Transactions on Computing for Healthcare 2 (2021), pp. 1–15. https://doi.org/10.1145/3453175
24. Terra, J.: Keras vs Tensorflow vs Pytorch: key differences among deep learning (2024). https://www.simplilearn.com/keras-vs-tensorflow-vs-pytorch-article#what_is_deep_learning%5C [Access 12 Apr 2024]
25. Towards Healthcare. chatbots for mental health and therapy market size envisioned at USD 6.51 Billion by 2032 (2023). https://www.towardshealthcare.com/insights/chatbots-formental-health-and-therapy-market [Access 30 May 2024]
26. World Health Organization. Mental disorders (2022). https://www.who.int/news-room/fact-sheets/detail/mentaldisorders [Access 19 May 2024]
27. Wysa. Mental health that meets people where they are (2024). https://www.wysa.com/ [Access 30 May 2024]
28. Wysa. Wysa: transforming mental health through AI-driven support (2023). https://emhicglobal.com/case-studies/ai/wysa-transforming-mental-health-through-ai-driven-support/ [Access 30 May 2024]
29. Youper.: Empathetic, safe, and clinically validated chatbot for mental healthcare (2024). https://www.youper.ai/ [Access 30 May 2024]

Enhancing Cybersecurity: Evaluation of GenAI Tools for the Improvement of Social Engineering Awareness

Ilona Veitaitė(✉)

Institute of Social Sciences and Applied Informatics, Vilnius University, Muitinės Street 8, 44280 Kaunas, Lithuania
ilona.veitaite@knf.vu.lt

Abstract. Social engineering is one of the major cybersecurity risks that exploit human psychology to deceive individuals into revealing sensitive information. Unlike cyberattacks targeting software vulnerabilities, these schemes manipulate emotions, trust, and authority. Common tactics include phishing, pretexting, baiting, and reverse social engineering, where attackers trick victims into seeking help. In recent years, social engineering remains widespread, responsible for a large share of cyber breaches, with a high number of businesses reporting at least one attack. Advanced techniques like deepfake technology and Generative Artificial Intelligence (GenAI) make these scams more convincing, increasing the challenge of distinguishing real from fraudulent interactions. Organizations must implement comprehensive training to mitigate risks, emphasizing skepticism and verification. GenAI tools play a vital role in strengthening social engineering awareness by automating phishing detection, behavioral analysis, and deepfake identification. AI-driven chatbots enhance security training, while threat intelligence platforms monitor social media for fraudulent activity. By integrating these AI solutions, organizations can better detect, prevent, and educate employees about evolving cyber threats. An important part of effectively leveraging AI in this context involves accurately calculating and managing token usage, ensuring that models can process complex communications efficiently without compromising analysis depth or performance.

Keywords: social engineering · cybersecurity · cyber-attack · awareness · token

1 Introduction

Cybersecurity is a growing concern in today's digital world, with individuals and organizations facing increasing threats. Phishing and social engineering are among the most prevalent, exploiting human trust to steal sensitive information. As technology advances, attackers use AI-driven phishing campaigns and deepfake technology, making these threats harder to detect [1].

Phishing involves deceptive emails, messages, or websites designed to trick victims into revealing personal data. Email phishing targets large groups, while spear phishing

K. Wącel (Ed.): BIS 2025 Workshops, LNBIP 568, pp. 28–39, 2026.
https://doi.org/10.1007/978-3-032-11651-2_3

tailors attacks to specific individuals or organizations. Whaling focuses on high-profile executives, smishing and vishing use texts and calls, and angler phishing exploits social media [2]. Modern phishing challenges stem from AI-generated attacks, rapid message distribution, and cross-border cybercrime. Deepfakes can mimic trusted individuals, and phishing techniques evolve to include Quick Response (QR) codes and instant messaging. These attacks cause financial losses, reputational damage, and erode trust in digital communication [3].

Countermeasures include public awareness, multi-factor authentication, advanced email filters, and global cybersecurity collaboration. Yet, human error remains the weakest link. Despite evolving security measures, lack of awareness and poor training make users vulnerable. This is evident, as cyberattacks cost over $400 billion globally, with 35% of breaches due to human error [4].

AI holds significant potential in enhancing social engineering awareness through various applications. By analyzing vast datasets, AI can identify patterns and anomalies indicative of social engineering attempts, such as phishing emails or fraudulent messages. This proactive approach enables the development of advanced threat detection systems that alert users to potential risks, thereby reducing the likelihood of successful attacks. Furthermore, AI-driven training programs can simulate realistic social engineering scenarios, providing users with hands-on experience in recognizing and responding to such threats. These immersive training methods have been shown to improve user vigilance and response times, contributing to a more security-aware culture within organizations [5, 6].

As AI technology becomes more accessible, cybercriminals are also leveraging it to craft more sophisticated social engineering attacks. For instance, AI-generated deepfake videos and voice cloning can convincingly impersonate trusted individuals, making it challenging for users to discern legitimate communications from malicious ones. This escalation underscores the need for continuous advancements in AI-based defense mechanisms and regular updates to training programs to address emerging threats. By staying informed about the evolving tactics employed by attackers, organizations can better equip their employees to recognize and counteract AI-enhanced social engineering schemes, thereby strengthening their overall cybersecurity posture [6, 7].

As organizations increasingly adopt AI-based solutions to strengthen defenses against social engineering attacks, it becomes essential to rigorously evaluate the effectiveness of these GenAI models. A critical factor in this evaluation is understanding how models process information, particularly through token usage. Tokens represent the basic units of text interpretation and generation for AI models, influencing both output accuracy and system performance. Variations in tokenization methods, such as Byte Pair Encoding (BPE) affect how models handle and analyze communication data. Inefficient token handling can lead to truncated outputs, incomplete threat simulations, or misinterpretations. Careful assessment of token efficiency, including external token counting beyond internal estimates, is vital to ensure consistent analysis and optimize resource use. By evaluating both token management and behavioral accuracy, organizations can select AI models that are not only effective in detecting social engineering attempts but also scalable, cost-efficient, and aligned with the evolving demands of cybersecurity resilience [8, 9].

2 Related Works

AI-based phishing detection and prevention techniques increasingly rely on hybrid machine learning (ML) and deep learning (DL) models, such as Convolutional Neural Network and Long Short-Term Memory (CNN-LSTM) and ensemble frameworks, which achieve high accuracy in identifying phishing emails, URLs, and websites [8, 9]. Multi-channel detection tools apply AI to email, SMS, and social media threats, with some deployed in real-world enterprise environments like browser plugins and adaptive filters [9]. However, adversarial AI techniques, particularly large language models (LLMs) used to craft sophisticated phishing emails, present significant challenges to existing defenses, requiring improvements in adversarial training and adaptive learning models [10, 11]. Deepfake-enhanced phishing further exacerbates risks, with real-world financial losses, such as a $25 million AI-generated scam, indicating that phishing detection systems must integrate AI-driven media forensics to analyze artifacts in voice and video attacks [11].

Despite advancements, challenges persist, including high false-positive rates that impact usability in corporate environments and evolving attacker tactics that bypass static AI models [9, 12]. Deepfake detection remains an area with limited enterprise adoption, despite promising AI techniques such as temporal coherence and feature inconsistency analysis to identify manipulated media [13]. Financial and healthcare sectors face the highest risks due to deepfake phishing's scalability and credibility, emphasizing the need for real-world-tested AI solutions that integrate detection, prevention, and behavioral analytics [13, 14]. Going forward, research must focus on strengthening adversarial resilience, refining explainable AI (XAI) to improve trust in automated phishing detection, and ensuring regulatory compliance while balancing security needs against AI's potential misuse in crafting advanced phishing campaigns [13, 15].

3 Impact of Social Engineering

Social engineering, in its simplest form, involves influencing individuals to take actions that may or may not align with their best interests. It is the practice of manipulating people, often through psychological tactics, to gain unauthorized access to systems, data, and sensitive information. Instead of relying on technical hacking methods, social engineering exploits human behavior to breach security measures. More specifically, it is a cyberattack strategy that deceives victims into believing the attacker is a trusted individual, leading them to share confidential details such as passwords or authorize financial transactions. With the rise of social media, these attacks have become more sophisticated, as attackers can easily gather personal or professional information to impersonate friends, family, or colleagues [16].

Social engineering poses a significant threat to businesses, particularly small and medium-sized enterprises (SMEs). Unlike traditional cyberattacks that exploit system vulnerabilities, these tactics target human psychology to compromise organizational security. Attackers employ various deceptive techniques to manipulate individuals into revealing sensitive data or carrying out harmful actions. As one of the most prevalent and effective methods of unauthorized access, social engineering – often combined with phishing – has led to substantial financial losses for organizations. Statistics highlight the alarming impact of such attacks, demonstrating their effectiveness in bypassing conventional security defenses: social engineering is behind 98% of all computer attacks [17]; over 70% of data breaches begin with phishing or social engineering attacks [18]; some 43% of phishing e-mails impersonate well-known entities, such as Microsoft [19]; SMEs with fewer than 100 employees are 3 times more likely to be the target of social engineering [20]; 43% of IT professionals targeted by social engineering in previous years [21]; a study by the Cyber Security Hub revealed that 3 out of 4 cybersecurity professionals considered social engineering or phishing attacks to be the "most dangerous" threat to their organization's cybersecurity [22]; the IBM report says that social engineering attacks can take up to 270 days to be detected and contained on average [23]; Social engineering attempts increased by more than 500% in the past few years [24].

4 AI Tools for Social Engineering Awareness

Social engineering attacks exploit human psychology to gain unauthorized access to systems and sensitive data. AI tools can help improve cybersecurity awareness by detecting, preventing, and educating users about these threats. Below are some AI-driven tools and methods that can be used for social engineering awareness. Based on the purpose and techniques of AI tools it is possible categorize them [8, 9]:

- AI-Powered Phishing Detection & Awareness, where Machine Learning Models: analyze email headers, content, and behavior to detect phishing attempts; Natural Language Processing (NLP): identifies suspicious language patterns in emails and messages; User Behavior Analysis: detects unusual login attempts or access behaviors; Phishing Simulations: sends mock phishing emails to train employees in identifying threats. Main techniques used: Spear Phishing Detection: AI scans for impersonation attempts targeting specific individuals; Deepfake Email & Voice Analysis: AI identifies deepfake emails and voice phishing (vishing); Automated Alerts & Responses: AI warns users in real time when suspicious emails are detected.
- AI-driven Chatbots for Security Training, where Conversational AI Training: engages users in simulated phishing and fraud scenarios; Gamification: makes security training interactive and memorable; Adaptive Learning: personalizes training based on user responses and behavior. Main techniques used: Real-time Threat Awareness: Chatbots provide security tips based on current attack trends; Scenario-based Training: Users interact with AI chatbots that mimic scammers to test their awareness; Feedback & Assessment: AI evaluates responses and provides corrective actions.
- AI-Based Deepfake Detection, where Face Recognition & Voice Analysis: AI analyzes facial expressions, speech, and inconsistencies in videos; Metadata & Pixel Analysis: detects tampering in digital files; Machine Learning on Audio & Video: identifies fake recordings used in social engineering scams. Main techniques used: Deepfake Awareness Training: Employees learn to identify manipulated media; Real-time Alerts: AI warns users about potentially fake calls or videos; Automated Social Media Monitoring: AI flags suspicious content spreading misinformation.

- Behavioral Analysis for Social Engineering Detection, where User Behavior Analytics (UBA): AI tracks login patterns, access times, and communication behaviors; Anomaly Detection: identifies deviations from normal user activities; Risk Scoring: assigns risk levels to user behavior to detect potential insider threats. Main techniques used: Social Engineering Attack Detection: AI flags suspicious actions (e.g., unusual requests for access); Voice & Text Analysis: Detects patterns of deception in communications; Fraud Prevention: AI stops unauthorized fund transfers by analyzing behavioral patterns.
- AI-Powered Social Media & OSINT (Open-Source Intelligence) Monitoring, where Social Media Scanning: AI detects fake profiles, impersonations, and scam campaigns; Data Leak Detection: identifies exposed credentials from past breaches; Threat Intelligence Correlation: AI cross-references dark web data with enterprise security logs. Main techniques used: Fake Profile Identification: AI flags social engineering attempts from fraudulent accounts; Automated Content Moderation: Prevents scams from spreading in corporate networks; Brand & Reputation Monitoring: AI tracks mentions of an organization in phishing or impersonation attempts.

GenAI models, can play a vital role in strengthening social engineering awareness by providing realistic, ethical simulations and educational resources. These tools can simulate phishing emails, create role-playing scenarios, and generate engaging educational content to help employees recognize and resist manipulation attempts. For example, AI can safely replicate the tactics of real attackers so employees can practice spotting red flags in a controlled setting. By generating convincing phishing messages – such as an "urgent" wire-transfer request that appears to come from the CEO – or by role-playing a chatty "customer-support agent" who tries to coax login credentials out of users, the model lets security teams run immersive simulations and live conversations that expose staff to current attack styles without risking actual harm [27, 28].

Beyond simulations, AI can be employed to analyze communication procedures for vulnerabilities and tailor training modules to specific roles within an organization. Generative model can write eye-catching slogans for posters, script short explainer videos, draft interactive quizzes, or even spin up a choose-your-own-adventure game where players navigate branching social-engineering scenarios. Because content is generated on demand, it can be tailored to finance, HR, or any other department – for instance, a story in which a "job applicant" tries to trick HR into downloading malware – ensuring each team rehearses the threats most likely to target them. This tailored approach ensures that employees receive highly relevant training, increasing the likelihood that they will respond appropriately to real-world threats [28, 29].

Moreover, AI tools can contribute to gamifying cybersecurity training, making learning more interactive and memorable. I can act as a security reviewer, scanning everyday workflows for weak spots and supplying constructive feedback after drills. It can highlight language in a customer-service script that an attacker might exploit (e.g., over-eager politeness or artificial urgency), score employee responses to mock phishing or vishing attempts, and suggest wording or procedural changes that make future slips less likely. By combining simulation, education, and continuous assessment, GenAI helps organizations build a culture that recognizes and resists social-engineering attacks before they succeed. Overall, integrating AI into social engineering awareness programs offers dynamic, personalized, and effective ways to build a more resilient organizational culture against cyber threats [27, 29].

An important element to support this strategy is the use of structured social engineering policies, which can be used as one or several documents in any organization. These documents include key policies such as Acceptable Use Policy (AUP), Social Engineering Awareness Policy, Information Security Policy, Incident Response Plan (IRP), Data Classification & Handling Policy, Email & Communication Policy, Security Awareness Training Program, and Third-Party Communication & Verification Policy. These policies define employee responsibilities, communication safeguards, incident reporting mechanisms, and guidelines for data handling, thereby laying a firm organizational foundation for social engineering resilience.

These social engineering policies create a consistent, enforceable baseline that shapes employee behavior before, during, and after exposure to simulated attacks or real-world threats. When integrated with AI-driven methods such as tailored phishing simulations, real-time feedback analysis, and adaptive training content generation, the policies ensure that awareness programs are not only reactive but also proactive, scalable, and continuously improving. By anchoring AI-enabled training within a strong policy framework, organizations can systematically enhance employee vigilance and create an enduring culture of cybersecurity awareness.

To ensure that AI-driven social engineering awareness initiatives deliver meaningful results, it is crucial to regularly evaluate the effectiveness of AI usage. Simply deploying simulations and training modules is not enough; organizations must analyze how well these tools improve user behavior and resilience against threats over time. Without structured evaluation, there is a risk that AI-generated training content may become stale, too predictable, or misaligned with evolving real-world tactics. Metrics such as employee response rates, error rates during simulations, and feedback from participants can help organizations refine and adjust their AI strategies to maintain training relevance and effectiveness.

One valuable but often overlooked aspect of AI evaluation is the analysis of token usage – the smallest units of text that AI models process when generating content. Studying token patterns can reveal whether the AI is producing sufficiently diverse and realistic phishing simulations or if it is overusing predictable structures and phrasing that employees might eventually recognize and dismiss without real learning. By analyzing token complexity, language diversity, and contextual relevance, security teams can fine-tune the AI's output to keep training scenarios authentic and challenging. Incorporating token analysis into the feedback loop ensures that AI remains a dynamic and evolving ally in the fight against social engineering threats.

5 Methodology for GenAI Model Evaluation

In today's cybersecurity landscape, social engineering attacks remain among the most insidious and effective threats to organizational security. Recognizing this, the Social Engineering Awareness Improvement Methodology was developed to provide a structured and measurable approach to leveraging GenAI models for enhancing employee resilience against such attacks. The methodology aligns with globally accepted standards like ISO/IEC 27001 and NIST SP 800-53, ensuring it is adaptable to a wide range of organizational cybersecurity frameworks. Rather than focusing solely on theoretical training, this approach emphasizes real-world simulation, dynamic content generation, and continuous skill reinforcement tailored to each organization's specific needs.

The methodology evaluates GenAI models across five key dimensions that are critical to detecting and mitigating social engineering threats: Phishing Simulation and Detection, Behavioral Pattern Recognition, Communication Analysis, Security Awareness Training Support, and Insider Threat Detection. Each dimension challenges the GenAI model through defined categories such as Multi-format Input Analysis, Accuracy in Contextual Detection, Structured Information Extraction, Contextual Search and Filtering, Response Time and Performance, and Awareness Visualization. Practical testing scenarios are used to probe the AI's ability to handle complex human-centric data. For instance, evaluators might ask, *"Can the model extract emotional manipulation indicators from a series of customer service chat logs?"* or *"How quickly can the model retrieve all internal emails containing urgency-based social engineering tactics?"* Such precise testing ensures a realistic evaluation of each model's operational readiness.

To enhance the fairness and transparency of the evaluation, token calculation mechanisms are incorporated. Tokens represent the units of text processed by the AI, influencing both model performance and cost-efficiency. During the evaluation, two token counting approaches are considered: the model's internal token calculation (when available) and standardized external measurements based on Byte Pair Encoding (BPE) methods, such as using OpenAI's tiktoken library. Because many models – including those from OpenAI (GPT), Google (Gemini), and Microsoft (Copilot) – may not accurately self-report token usage, external tokenizers ensure that the evaluation of processing efficiency, particularly in multi-scenario or large dataset conditions, remains consistent and credible [30].

Furthermore, the methodology is not static. It encourages dynamic, scenario-based training exercises that adapt over time based on employee performance and evolving threat landscapes. For example, after an initial phishing simulation, employees' responses can be analyzed by the GenAI to identify weaknesses. The AI can then generate customized follow-up modules, such as a new role-play where a "vendor support agent" attempts to gain unauthorized system access. Evaluators might additionally pose questions such as "Can the model generate a department-specific training module based on prior phishing susceptibility rates?" thereby testing the system's ability to support continuous, personalized awareness development.

By embedding GenAI evaluation within a broader cybersecurity framework, organizations move beyond traditional static learning approaches toward a model of continuous learning and proactive defense. The methodology offers a systematic path to build cyber resilience, combining technical accuracy, human behavior understanding, resource efficiency (through token monitoring), and adaptive training development. As AI continues to evolve, methodologies like this ensure that its integration into cybersecurity strategies is responsible, effective, and fully aligned with protecting both organizational assets and human factors from the rising tide of social engineering threats.

6 GenAI Models Evaluation

In this experiment, GPT, Gemini, Copilot models were subjected to a series of tests to evaluate their performance. GPT, Gemini, and Copilot AI models are ideal candidates for social engineering awareness experiments due to their advanced natural language processing capabilities, broad accessibility, and diverse model architectures. GPT (ChatGPT), developed by OpenAI, excels at generating human-like responses, simulating realistic phishing messages, and analyzing conversational patterns with high contextual understanding. Gemini, powered by Google's Pathways Language Model (PaLM) architecture, offers strong integration with real-time web data, making it effective for detecting emerging social engineering tactics and analyzing complex communication datasets. Copilot, based on OpenAI's Codex and integrated with Microsoft's ecosystem, provides specialized strengths in code interpretation and structured logic processing, which can be adapted for simulating technical pretexting attacks and automating policy enforcement testing. Together, these models represent a broad spectrum of capabilities, ensuring comprehensive coverage of different social engineering attack vectors and response scenarios during evaluation [31, 32]. Each model was presented with six prompts, one per each category. The queries were submitted via web applications of mentioned models.

- *Can the model extract phishing indicators from a.msg or.eml file?*
- *Can the model highlight social engineering tactics (urgency, authority, fear) within a simulated email?*
- *Can the model extract sender, recipient, and flagged content from email chains?*
- *How quickly can it identify insider-related risks across 500MB of communication logs?*
- *How fast can the model analyze* 1 GB *of training feedback data?*
- *Can the model generate a graph of phishing susceptibility over time by department?*

The objective of this experiment was to develop and implement a methodology for evaluating the effectiveness of GenAI models in supporting social engineering awareness and training efforts within organizational cybersecurity frameworks. Hypotheses: H1: Different GenAI models will generate varied responses to identical prompts due to differences in their underlying architectures, tokenization methods, training datasets, and generation strategies, leading to observable discrepancies in content, structure, or interpretation. H2: Certain GenAI models, particularly those optimized for conversational accuracy, will demonstrate a higher likelihood of requesting prompt clarification compared to models with more deterministic or code-focused outputs, reflecting differences in interaction design and user intent recognition.

The study uses prompts derived from each category defined in methodology description. Before starting the prompts, file of organization policies is given to each GenAImodel. This file includes key policies (mentioned in section four), samples, with their general purposes and main points of each, ten pages in total. Each prompt was submitted in English and delivered sequentially to each model, accompanied by a uniform preamble. Models were instructed to provide responses that were specific, contextually relevant, and free from extraneous generalizations or conclusions. Concise explanations were permitted only when the prompt involved ambiguous or complex elements requiring clarification, and such explanations were to be offered exclusively upon explicit request, not through autonomous interpretation. Each prompt was accompanied by the following uniform preamble: *You are tasked with acting as an experienced IT security specialist (CISO) responsible for managing and mitigating cyber-attacks by analyzing available information related to a cyber-incident. Before starting, familiarize yourself thoroughly with the provided Social Engineering Policies document, as it will serve as an essential reference for your decisions and evaluations. When responding to the given question or scenario, be highly specific, remain fully aligned with the context, and do not introduce any additional generalizations or independent conclusions. You must focus solely on the precise content of the prompt. Please answer this question: <question text>*

Table 1. Input and Output Token calculation per model (BPE)

?N	Input	GPT Output	Gemini Output	Copilot Output
1	21	245	135	298
2	25	180	108	451
3	20	180	98	487
4	21	187	37	416
5	19	195	19	404
6	19	199	24	378

Table 1 presents input and output token calculation per model (BPE) of each GenAI model used in the experiment. GenAI models: GPT, Gemini, and Copilot were evaluated on their ability to support social engineering awareness efforts within an organizational cybersecurity framework. The results confirmed Hypothesis H1: the models generated varied responses to identical prompts, reflecting differences in their architectures and response strategies. Gemini produced the most concise outputs with minimal token usage, closely adhering to the provided policies but offering limited elaboration. GPT balanced policy-focused answers with thoughtful descriptions of missing data and model limitations, demonstrating higher contextual awareness. Copilot, while also grounded in the policy document, supplemented its responses with examples and suggestions, reflecting a more interpretive approach.

The findings also supported Hypothesis H2: GPT and Gemini, optimized for conversational accuracy, were more attentive to contextual clarifications, whereas Copilot focused more deterministically on the prompts, often proposing potential methods beyond the immediate policy content. Overall, the experiment highlighted the importance of selecting a GenAI model based on the desired balance between strict policy adherence, depth of reasoning, and the need for proactive clarification or extrapolation when addressing cybersecurity and social engineering scenarios.

The experiment emphasizes that GenAI models differ significantly in token efficiency, contextual depth, and security alignment – Gemini favors brevity, GPT balances completeness with policy compliance, and Copilot delivers detailed but costly outputs. These variations highlight the importance of systematic evaluation through token tracking and scenario-based testing, as well as ongoing refinement, feedback, disciplined policy use, and shared threat intelligence to build sustainable defenses against social engineering.

7 Conclusions

Social engineering remains a dominant cybersecurity threat because it exploits human judgment – the most unpredictable component in any defense system. The rise of AI-driven techniques, such as deepfakes and sophisticated phishing scams, has made these attacks more convincing and harder to detect. Despite advancements in cybersecurity measures, human error remains a significant vulnerability, with phishing and social engineering responsible for a large percentage of cyber breaches. AI-powered chatbots and training simulations provide interactive learning experiences that improve employee awareness and response to phishing attempts. AI-based monitoring tools help organizations identify fraudulent activities across emails, social media, and corporate networks.

GenAI tools offer promising solutions by automating realistic phishing simulations, detecting behavioral anomalies, and creating adaptive, role-specific training content. The research confirms that AI-driven mechanisms – from dynamic chatbots and deepfake detectors to real-time threat monitoring – significantly enhance an organization's ability to inoculate users against modern attack techniques. Crucially, the integration of these capabilities with foundational governance structures such as Acceptable-Use Policies and Incident Response Plans ensures that AI not only simulates threats but actively reinforces policy-driven security behaviors, creating a resilient feedback loop between users, technology, and organizational rules.

The study also highlights that not all GenAI models are created equal. GPT, Gemini, and Copilot exhibit notable differences in token efficiency, contextual depth, and adherence to security policies. Gemini prioritizes brevity at the cost of nuance, GPT achieves a balance between completeness and policy alignment, while Copilot offers detailed outputs with higher token consumption. These variations underscore the need for systematic model evaluation – using external token counting and scenario-based accuracy testing – to avoid performance blind spots and cost inefficiencies. Ultimately, sustainable defenses against social engineering will depend on continuous AI refinement, real-world performance feedback, disciplined policy integration, and collaborative threat intelligence sharing.

Declaration on Generative AI. During the preparation of this work, the author used GPT-40 and Grammarly in order to: Grammar and spelling check. After using these tools, the author reviewed and edited the content as needed and takes full responsibility for the publication's content.

References

1. Lewallen, J.: Emerging technologies and problem definition uncertainty: the case of cybersecurity. Regul. Gov. **15**(4), 1035–1052 (2020). https://doi.org/10.1111/rego.12341

2. Craigen, D., Diakun-Thibault, N., Purse, R.: Defining cybersecurity. Technol. Innov. Manag. Rev. **4**(10), 13–21 (2014). https://doi.org/10.22215/timreview/835
3. Schatz, D., Bashroush, R., Wall, J.: Towards a more representative definition of cyber security. J. Digit. Forensics Secur. Law (2017). https://doi.org/10.15394/jdfsl.2017.1476
4. Walker, E., Witkowski, D., Benczik, S., Jarrin, P.: Cybersecurity –the Human Factor. Prioritizing People Solutions to improve the cyber resiliency of the Federal workforce. https://csrc.nist.gov/CSRC/media/Events/FISSEA-30th-AnnualConference/documents/FISSEA2017_Witkowski_Benczik_Jarrin_Walker_Materials_Final.pdf
5. Cahill, J.: AI is Amplifying Social Engineering. INFIMA Security, 14 July 2023. https://infimasec.com/blog/ai-and-social-engineering/
6. Sjouwerman, S.: AI Tools Have Increased the Sophistication of Social Engineering Attacks. KnowBe4, 6 August 2024. https://blog.knowbe4.com/ai-tools-have-increased-sophistication-of-social-engineering-attacks
7. Concannon, M.: AI in Social Engineering: The Next Generation of Cyber Threats. Ntiva, 16 July 2024. https://www.ntiva.com/blog/ai-social-engineering-attacks
8. Author, D. G.-T. E. C.: AI Tokens Explained: Complete Guide to Usage, Optimization & Costs. Deepak Gupta | AI & Cybersecurity Innovation Leader | Founder's Journey From Code to Scale, 28 January 28 2025. https://guptadeepak.com/complete-guide-to-ai-tokens-understanding-optimization-and-cost-management/
9. Salvator, D.: Explaining Tokens – the language and currency of AI | NVIDIA blog. NVIDIA Blog, 18 March 2025. https://blogs.nvidia.com/blog/ai-tokens-explained/
10. Sultana, R., Rahman, M.A., Khan, M.I.: Hybrid model based phishing websites detection using deep learning technique. In: 2023 26th International Conference on Computer and Information Technology (ICCIT) (2023). https://doi.org/10.1109/iccit60459.2023.10441639
11. Kamble, N., Mishra, N.: Securing cyberspace: unveiling phishing attacks through deep neural networks for enhanced detection. In: 2024 International Conference on Advancements in Smart, Secure and Intelligent Computing (ASSIC), pp. 1–5 (2024). https://doi.org/10.1109/assic60049.2024.10508000
12. Riurean, P., Bolog, G., Riurean, S.: The rise of sophisticated phishing. How AI fuels cybercrime. J. Digit. Sci. **6**(2), 15–25 (2024). https://doi.org/10.33847/2686-8296.6.2_2
13. Jampani, S.K.: Social Engineering 2.0 deepfake and deep learning-based cyber-attacks (Phishing). Int. J. Multidiscip. Res. **7**(1) (2025). https://doi.org/10.36948/ijfmr.2025.v07i01.35527
14. Tang, L., Mahmoud, Q.H.: A deep learning-based framework for phishing website detection. IEEE Access **10**, 1509–1521 (2021). https://doi.org/10.1109/access.2021.3137636
15. Fakhouri, H.N., Alhadidi, B., Omar, K., Makhadmeh, S.N., Hamad, F., Halalsheh, N.Z.: AI-driven solutions for social engineering attacks: detection, prevention, and response. In: 2024 2nd International Conference on Cyber Resilience (ICCR), pp. 1–8 (2024). https://doi.org/10.1109/iccr61006.2024.10533010
16. Mathew, A., Federico, R.: Phishing 2.0: leveraging cyber threat intelligence to combat deepfake-enhanced social engineering. Int. J. Innov. Res. Sci. Eng. Technol. **14**(02) (2025). https://doi.org/10.15680/ijirset.2025.1402003
17. Sanchez-Paniagua, M., Fernandez, E.F., Alegre, E., Al-Nabki, W., Gonzalez-Castro, V.: Phishing URL detection: a real-case scenario through login URLs. IEEE Access **10**, 42949–42960 (2022). https://doi.org/10.1109/access.2022.3168681
18. Washo, A.H.: An interdisciplinary view of social engineering: a call to action for research. Comput. Hum. Behav. Rep. **4**, 100126 (2021). https://doi.org/10.1016/j.chbr.2021.100126
19. Reed, C.: 30 Social Engineering Statistics – 2023. Firewall Times, 18 September 2023. https://firewalltimes.com/social-engineering-statistics/

20. Social engineering, an invisible threat: trends and developments. Altospam, 27 November2023. https://www.altospam.com/en/news/social-engineering-an-invisible-threat-trends-and-developments/. Accessed 2 Mar 2025
21. Schutz, M.: Warning: 43% of Recent Phishing Attacks Impersonate Microsoft. Pktech, 13 November 2024. https://pktech.net/blog/2021/08/warning-43-of-recent-phishing-attacks-impersonate-microsoft
22. Understanding social engineering and small businesses – Intelligent SME.tech., 21 March 2024. https://www.intelligentsme.tech/2024/03/21/understanding-social-engineering-and-small-businesses/
23. Sjouwerman, S.: Social Engineering is a Core Element of Nearly Every Cyber Attack. KnowBe4, 29 April 2022. https://blog.knowbe4.com/social-engineering-is-a-core-element-of-nearly-every-cyber-attack
24. Powell, O.: Social engineering "most dangerous" threat, say 75% of security professionals. Cyber Security Hub. Cyber Security Hub, 8 May 2022. https://www.cshub.com/attacks/news/social-engineering-most-dangerous-threat-say-75-of-security-professionals. Accessed 3 Mar 2025
25. IBM Report: Consumers pay the price as data Breach Costs Reach All-Time High. IBM Newsroom, 27 July 2022. https://newsroom.ibm.com/2022-07-27-IBM-Report-Consumers-Pay-the-Price-as-Data-Breach-Costs-Reach-All-Time-High
26. Bonnie, E.: 60+ Social Engineering Statistics. Secureframe, 31 December 2024. https://secureframe.com/blog/social-engineering-statistics. Accessed 2025
27. Schmitt, M., Flechais, I.: Digital deception: generative artificial intelligence in social engineering and phishing. Artif. Intell. Rev. **57**(12) (2024). https://doi.org/10.1007/s10462-024-10973-2
28. Fujihira, K.: Systematic method for identifying unsuitable land for development: biodiversity, disaster risk, and topography. Acad. Environ. Sci. Sustain. **2**(2) (2025). https://doi.org/10.20935/AcadEnvSci7647
29. Steinmetz, K.F., Holt, T.J., Brewer, C.G.: Developing and implementing social engineering-prevention policies: a qualitative study. Secur. J. **37**, 599–617 (2024). https://doi.org/10.1057/s41284-023-00385-2
30. Openai: GitHub - openai/tiktoken: tiktoken is a fast BPE tokeniser for use with OpenAI's models. GitHub (n.d.). https://github.com/openai/tiktoken
31. Hochmair, H.H., Juhász, L., Kemp, T.: Correctness comparison of ChatGPT-4, Gemini, Claude-3, and Copilot for spatial tasks. Trans. GIS **28**(7), 2219–2231 (2024). https://doi.org/10.1111/tgis.13233
32. Salman, I.M., Ameer, O.Z., Khanfar, M.A., Hsieh, Y.: Artificial intelligence in healthcare education: evaluating the accuracy of ChatGPT, Copilot, and Google Gemini in cardiovascular pharmacology. Front. Med. **12** (2025). https://doi.org/10.3389/fmed.2025.1495378

Blockchain-Based Solution for Decentralized Identity Aligned with EU and W3C Standards

Laura Atmanavičiūtė(✉), Mykolas Rutkauskas, Aristidas Lukas Končius, Gintarė Košubienė, and Saulius Masteika

Kaunas Faculty, Vilnius University, Muitinės g. 8, 44280 Kaunas, Lithuania
{laura.atmanaviciute,gintare.kosubiene, saulius.masteika}@knf.vu.lt, {mykolas.rutkauskas, aristidas.koncius}@knf.stud.vu.lt

Abstract. As governments and organizations increasingly explore digital identity systems, decentralized digital identity (DDI) has emerged as a compelling alternative to centralized models, offering enhanced privacy, user autonomy, and resilience. A critical challenge, however, lies in identifying blockchain architectures that align with regulatory standards while preserving decentralization and scalability. This paper examines the key requirements outlined by EU regulations and W3C standards for DDI implementation. It conducts a comparative evaluation of existing decentralized identity solutions and analyzes blockchain platforms - Hyperledger Indy (permissioned), Ethereum Layer-2 and Polygon (permissionless). The study finds that Polygon, adapted into a permissioned configuration, can support essential privacy-preserving technologies such as Zero-Knowledge Proofs (ZKP), Verifiable Credentials (VC), and Decentralized Identifiers (DID), providing scalability and interoperability. Based on these findings, the paper recommends Polygon as a suitable foundation for standards-compliant DDI systems, provided it is implemented with appropriate permissioned controls. This work contributes to the ongoing research on aligning blockchain infrastructure with regulatory and technical requirements of digital identity.

Keywords: Decentralized digital identity · Blockchain selection · Permissioned blockchain · Permissionless blockchain · Hyperledger Indy · Polygon · Ethereum

1 Introduction

As digital identity adoption increases, governments and organizations worldwide are transitioning toward digital identity solutions to enhance security, efficiency, and user convenience [1]. However, traditional centralized identity management systems often struggle to address key concerns such as privacy, user control, and resilience to cyberattacks [2–6]. Consequently, decentralized digital identity (DDI) systems leveraging blockchain technology have emerged as promising alternatives, offering enhanced security, privacy, and autonomy [2]. These decentralized approaches hold significant potential for various sectors, including banking, healthcare, e-commerce, and public administration [1].

K. Wącel (Ed.): BIS 2025 Workshops, LNBIP 568, pp. 40–52, 2026.
https://doi.org/10.1007/978-3-032-11651-2_4

Despite their advantages, implementing decentralized identities faces challenges, particularly in selecting appropriate blockchain architectures [5–7]. The debate between permissioned and permissionless blockchains is critical in this decision [8]. Permissionless blockchains, such as Polygon, offer transparency, decentralization, and resistance to manipulation but may face compliance issues with data protection regulations like GDPR [9, 10]. In contrast, permissioned blockchains, such as Hyperledger Indy, provide enhanced control and regulatory compliance at the potential expense of scalability and decentralization [8, 11]. Balancing decentralization and regulatory compliance remain a key issue.

Previous studies highlight the benefits of decentralized identity, such as improved privacy and user control [2, 4, 5]. Regulatory alignment challenges, particularly concerning General Data Protection Regulation (GDPR) and eIDAS 2.0, have also been emphasized [6, 12], along with the implications of new standards introduced by the European Digital Identity (EUDI) Regulation and eIDAS 2.0 [12–14]. Technical analyses of permissioned and permissionless blockchains illustrate trade-offs between trust, performance, scalability, and privacy-preserving technologies ZKP [4, 7–9, 15]. Nevertheless, a definitive recommendation on which blockchain architecture best fulfils EU regulatory requirements and performance expectations remains unresolved. This gap motivates the present work.

This paper aims to evaluate and recommend a suitable blockchain solution for DDI systems by analyzing EU and W3C regulatory and standardization requirements and assessing permissioned and permissionless blockchain architectures. The research objectives include analyzing regulatory compliance criteria, comparing decentralized identity projects, assessing blockchain architectures, and recommending an optimal blockchain solution. Additionally, a proof-of-concept implementation is presented to validate the findings.

This study explores two hypotheses:

- **H1:** Blockchain technology can be effectively utilized in digital identity systems to enhance security, privacy, and interoperability while meeting regulatory and standardization requirements.
- **H2:** DDI systems can be successfully implemented on permissionless blockchains, ensuring compliance with regulatory standards.

The main contributions of this paper are as follows: (1) it translates the key requirements of GDPR, eIDAS 2.0 and the W3C DID/VC specifications into a concise set of evaluation criteria (Fig. 2); (2) it applies those criteria to compare real-world DDI deployments and three candidate blockchains, as summarized in Tables 1, 2 and 3; and (3) it illustrates the findings with a small proof-of-concept test showing that a permissioned Polygon ID instance can issue credentials in under two seconds on ordinary hardware - practical evidence of using Polygon as a compliant platform for digital-identity systems.

The paper is structured as follows: Sect. 2 outlines the methodology. Section 3 presents the analysis of regulatory and technical aspects, including the comparative evaluation and recommended blockchain platform. Section 4 describes the proof-of-concept experiment. Section 5 concludes with key insights and future research directions.

2 Methodology

This study adopts a systematic, five-phase approach to identify the most suitable blockchain type and platform for DDI systems (Fig. 1).

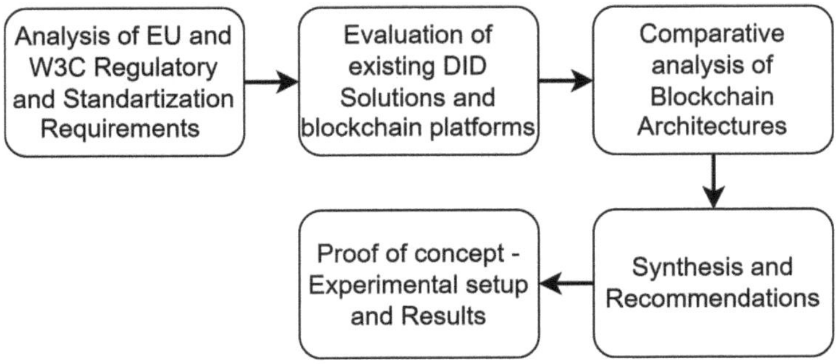

Fig. 1. Methodology for Blockchain Type and Platform Selection in DDI

In Phase 1, the study begins with a focused analysis of the primary regulations that govern digital identity in Europe, namely the GDPR, the amended eIDAS 2.0 framework, and the W3C recommendations for DIDs and VCs. Key articles from these instruments were mapped to three evaluation categories: privacy, security and interoperability. To understand how those legal requirements interact with blockchain design, a targeted reading of recent technical literature was carried out, concentrating on works that discuss GDPR constraints on immutable ledgers [16], eIDAS-driven security controls [17] and privacy enhancing mechanisms available in permissioned blockchains [18–21]. The outcome of this phase is a set of compliance and performance criteria, summarized in Fig. 2.

Phase 2 analyzes DDI initiatives from both government and private sectors. Solutions are retained if they report the use of at least one privacy primitive (Zero-Knowledge Proofs (ZKP), Verifiable Credentials (VC) or Decentralized Identifiers (DID)) and disclose their underlying blockchain layer. These projects are compared on five selection criteria derived from Phase 1: regulatory fit, scalability, privacy features, interoperability and cost efficiency.

Phase 3 undertakes the side-by-side assessment of permissioned and permissionless blockchains. Quantitative figures for throughput, latency and transaction cost are taken from public block-explorer APIs (Polygonscan, Indyscan) and, where available, peer-reviewed benchmarks. Qualitative attributes such as consensus mechanism, privacy support and governance model are verified against official protocol documentation. Any conflicting data are resolved by checking a second independent source; the final values reported in Tables 1, 2 and 3 therefore represent cross-validated information.

In Phase 4, findings from Phase 3 are synthesized to identify the platform that best balances regulatory compliance with performance and privacy. The analysis also highlights open questions for future research.

Phase 5 conducts a small-scale implementation exercise to demonstrate practical feasibility of the recommended platform and to confirm that the documented figures can be reproduced in a controlled setting.

3 Analysis of Regulatory and Technical Aspects in DDI Systems

The selection of a suitable blockchain type is fundamental to the development of digital identity frameworks, which aim to provide secure, user-controlled, and portable identity solutions. Regulatory frameworks, including the EU GDPR and the EIDAS 2.0, along with W3C standards, are instrumental in shaping blockchain architectures to ensure compliance with legal and standardization requirements. These regulations impose strict requirements for privacy, security, and accountability, necessitating a detailed evaluation of blockchain models and platforms. Figure 2 illustrates how the regulatory landscape provides a foundational framework for identifying blockchain architectures that ensure security, compliance, and scalability in digital identity ecosystems while mitigating challenges posed by non-compliant models.

GDPR creates major limits for blockchain implementations, particularly due to blockchain's immutability and decentralized structure. Key GDPR challenges include the right to erasure (Article 17), conflicting with blockchain immutability; data minimization principles (Article 5), which require limiting personal data storage; data protection by design (Article 25), necessitating privacy-centric architectures; accountability for cross-border data handling (Article 3), which is complicated by blockchain's decentralized nature; controlled processing relationships (Article 28), difficult to define in decentralized systems; and mandatory traceability and record-keeping obligations (Article 30), posing further complexities [16]. In practice these issues are mitigated by keeping personal attributes off-chain and proving their integrity on-chain through hash anchors and selective-disclosure Zero Knowledge Proofs.

Similarly, eIDAS 2.0 emphasizes stringent privacy, security, and accountability requirements, complicating permissionless blockchain adoption [17]. These requirements include privacy-preserving design ensuring logical separation of personal data processing (Article 5a), robust cyber-incident management demanding rapid breach response (Article 5e), regular vulnerability assessments (Article 12a), comprehensive auditability, and controlled access to network services, each presenting significant implementation challenges for public blockchain solutions. Because node operators on a permissionless network cannot be compelled to apply access controls or security patches, a supervisory layer is usually required when eIDAS compliance is sought.

Private permissioned blockchains effectively address these regulatory requirements, offering tailored solutions with enhanced privacy, security protocols, and regulatory compliance mechanisms [18]. Advanced technical measures include role-based access control for effective data governance, ZKP enabling selective disclosure of essential data, homomorphic encryption for secure data handling, and off-chain storage of DID to limit on-chain exposure of sensitive data [19]. When combined with W3C practices, such as pair-wise DIDs, automated key rotation, secure recovery workflows and revocation registries, these blockchains align closely with W3C standards, providing DID

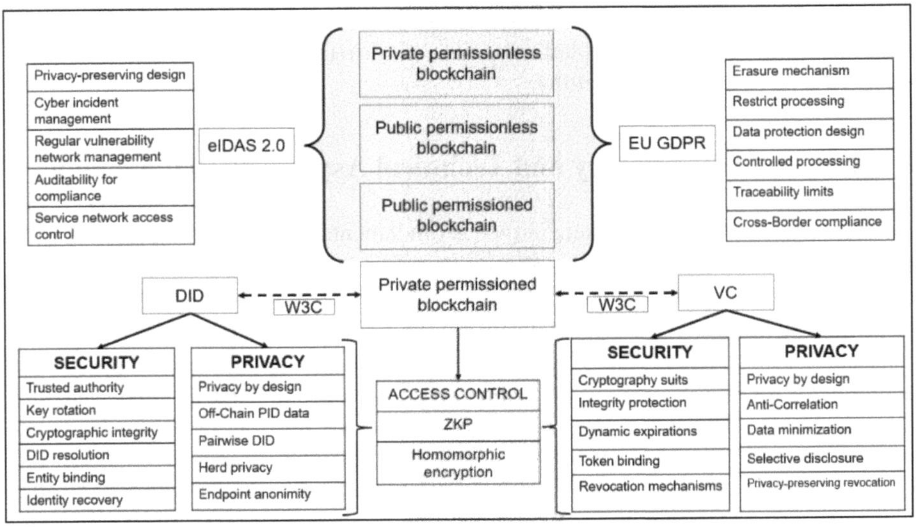

Fig. 2. Fundamental Factors for Identifying Blockchain in Digital Identity Framework

traceability, automated key rotation, secure identity recovery, pairwise DID implementations, privacy-preserving revocation mechanisms, and data authenticity protections for VCs [20, 21].

3.1 Comparative Analysis of DDI Solutions

To determine the most suitable blockchain type and platform for DDI systems, a comparative analysis of both start-up and government-led solutions was conducted. The evaluation focused on regulatory and technical features such as support for ZKP, VC, DID, blockchain, use case and KYC/AML application. Key start-up projects are summarized in Table 1.

While start-up solutions tend to emphasize innovation and flexibility, often prioritizing scalability, privacy features, and user-centric design - government initiatives focus more heavily on regulatory control, institutional trust, and integration with existing public infrastructure. This difference in priorities highlights the contrasting approaches to decentralized identity development across sectors and sets the stage for the overview of government-led implementations presented in Table 2.

The findings show a clear divide: start-ups typically adopt permissionless blockchains like Ethereum and Polygon, drawn by scalability and interoperability. Polygon addresses Ethereum's throughput limitations and is favored for high demand use cases [37]. Governments, on the other hand, prefer permissioned platforms such as Hyperledger Indy, which offer greater control and compliance capabilities [38, 39].

Solutions that integrate at least three core components - ZKP, VC, DID, and selective disclosure - demonstrate stronger alignment with regulatory and privacy requirements. Examples include Anima, Sovrin, Privado ID, zk.me, Bhutan NDI, and QuarkID. Bhutan's recent transition from Hyperledger Indy to Polygon in 2024 underscores a broader shift toward more scalable and flexible blockchain options.

Table 1. Overview of Start-Up DDI Solutions [22–31]

Solution	ZKP/Disclosure	VC/DID	DID Storage	Blockchain	Use Case & KYC/AML
Lissi Wallet	CL ZKP, Attr. proofs	W3C VC, did:indy	Wallet	Indy	SSI wallet (eID, KYC)
Anima	Encryption, selective data	SSI creds, Eth DID	Off-chain (Aleph.im) [36]	Ethereum	Portable Web3 KYC (Synaps)
Civic Pass	ZKP explored, Age/location	Reusable VCs, did:ethr	Civic wallet/cloud	Ethereum, Solana	On-chain compliance, KYC docs
Veramo	Plugin based disclosure	JWT/JSON-LD, Multi-DID	N/A	Agnostic	SDK for SSI agents
Sovrin	AnonCreds, selective	AnonCreds, did:indy	Edge wallet/Ledger	Hyperledger Indy	Public SSI network
Privado ID	zk-SNARKs, ZK proofs	Polygon ID VC, did:iden3, did:polygonid	Off-chain	Polygon (private)	Privacy focused SSI, Verite KYC
Solana ID	ZkPass, no PII revealed	VC stamps, did:sol	On-chain	Solana	Sybil-resist. ID, zkPass Gov ID
Keyring	ZK attestations	W3C VC, did:ethr	Off-chain verif., on-chain	Ethereum	Institutional DeFi KYC
Holonym	ZK reveal attributes	DID creds	Off-chain ZK, on-chain	Ethereum, Polygon	Proof-of-personhood, Gov ID
zk.me	zk-SNARKs, selective ZK	Polygon ID VC	Off-chain Polygon wallet	zkSync, Polygon	FATF-compliant zkKYC
Dock	BBS + selective proofs	VC, did:dock	On-chain	Dock	SSI platform (ID credentials)

Given these trends and the EUDI Wallet's emphasis on interoperability and selective disclosure, the analysis proceeds with a focused comparison of Hyperledger Indy, Polygon and Ethereum to assess their respective suitability for DDI frameworks.

3.2 Comparative Analysis of Blockchains

Hyperledger Indy, Polygon, and Ethereum-based solutions represent distinct approaches to supporting DDI systems. Hyperledger Indy is a permissioned blockchain designed specifically for self-sovereign identity (SSI). It offers native support for W3C-compliant DID and VC and includes privacy-preserving features such as ZKP and selective disclosure [40, 41]. Public-network measurements typically report throughputs below 300 TPS, yet laboratory benchmarks on a five-node c5.4xlarge cluster running Indy v1.16 with state pruning and batched writes have demonstrated sustained rates of 10× the throughput of the original Indy ledger [47].

Table 2. Overview of Government-Led DDI Solutions [32–36]

Solution	ZKP/Disclosure	VC/DID	DID Storage	Blockchain	KYC/AML	Use Case & KYC/AML
Estonia e-Residency	None, full disclosure	X.509 certs (non W3C)	Central PKI, smartcard	None	Government ID vetting	Digital ID for non-residents, Govt ID
Bhutan NDI	AnonCreds, zk-SNARK	W3C VC (CREDEBL), did:polygon	Govt-managed ledger	Polygon (private)	Biometric NID enrollment	National biometric ID (NID enrollment)
QuarkID (Buenos Aires)	zkSNARK proofs	W3C VC, did:ethr	On-chain zkRollup (zkSync Era)	zkSync L2 (public)	Gov records as credententials	Municipal SSI, Gov credentials
BC Wallet (Canada)	CL ZKP (AnonCreds)	Hyperledger VC, did:sov	Public permissioned ledger	Hyperledger Indy	Yes, provincial ID, licenses	Provincial digital wallet (IDs/licenses)
Singapore sgID	Partial disclosure	Govt-issued attributes	Central trust server (MyInfo)	None	National DB "MyInfo"	National ID selective data sharing
Irma/Yivi (NL)	Idemix ZKP	Attribute credentials	User device (attributes/ZK proofs)	None (peer to peer)	Yes	Open-source SSI attribute verification
Swiss e-ID (draft)	SSI, ZKP	Planned W3C VC/EU DID	Decentralized (user-controlled)	TBD	State-issued ID credentials	National e-ID, State-issued credentials
Findynet (Finland)	AnonCreds ZKP	Hyperledger VC, did:indy	Consortium ledger	Hyperledger Indy	Gov and bank IDs	Cooperative SSI (gov and bank credentials)

Polygon, by contrast, is a permissionless Ethereum Layer-2 network built for scalability, achieving up to 65,000 transactions per second (TPS) with low fees [37, 43]. Real-world deployments already prove that Polygon can run selective-disclosure proofs at scale. Bhutan's National Digital Identity issues VCs on a permissioned Polygon chain and uses Groth16 ZKPs for age and residence checks without exposing source attributes [33]. Buenos Aires' QuarkID adopts zk-SNARK proofs so municipal services can verify tax status while hiding salary data [32]. Holonym links government IDs to DeFi wallets with a proof-of-personhood ZKP that blocks Sybil attacks yet keeps full identity off-chain [30]. These cases demonstrate that Polygon-based ZKP circuits and W3C VCs are already operating in production, supporting this paper's recommendation for a privacy-preserving, Polygon-centred DDI stack. Ethereum Layer-2 solutions such as zkSync and Optimism provide similar benefits via rollups, offering modular scalability and strong interoperability with Ethereum [44].

Ethereum 2.0 introduces a proof-of-stake (PoS) consensus via the Beacon Chain and future sharding. The current PoS main-net processes around 15–20 TPS, as shown in Etherscan, while engineering targets range from 20 000 to 100 000 TPS once full sharding is active [48]. However, identity-related features remain reliant on application-layer solutions and upcoming ZKP upgrades.

Table 3 summarized the comparison across key criteria.

Table 3. Comparative Analysis of Hyperledger Indy and Polygon

Aspect	Hyperledger Indy [39, 40, 45]	Polygon [37, 43, 46]	Ethereum Layer-2 [44]	Ethereum 2.0 [44, 48]
Consensus mechanism	RBFT (permissioned)	Proof-of-Stake (PoS)	Rollups (ZK & Optimistic)	PoS (Beacon Chain)
Scalability	~3 000 TPS	~65,000 TPS	Thousands (varies by solution)	~15–20 TPS
Transaction cost	Medium (node & consensus overhead)	Low (avg. ~$0.013)	Low (off-chain processing)	Medium/Variable
Privacy	Native ZK Proof	Third-party ZK integrations	ZK Rollups and third-party integrations	Limited, future upgrades (ZK)
Interoperability	DID/VC standards, identity-focused	High (Ethereum-compatible)	High (Ethereum-compatible)	High (EVM-compatible chains)
Identity management	Native (W3C DID, VC)	Third-party solutions (CREDEBL)	Third-party/Ethereum-based solutions	Ethereum-based DID solutions

Despite its strong compliance capabilities, Hyperledger Indy's limited scalability restricts large-scale deployments. Ethereum Layer-2 networks and Polygon offer greater scalability, interoperability, and cost-efficiency, making them more adaptable to evolving identity ecosystems. Among them, Polygon stands out for its balance of speed, cost, and ecosystem maturity. It is thus recommended as the most practical platform for DDI, especially where large-scale, interoperable, and economically viable identity solutions are required.

3.3 Synthesis and Recommendation of Blockchain Platform for Digital Identity

The comparative analysis reveals critical differences in how privacy, regulatory alignment, and scalability are addressed by the evaluated blockchain platforms. Hyperledger Indy provides robust governance and privacy mechanisms but faces scalability and cost limitations. Ethereum Layer-2 solutions offer enhanced scalability and interoperability; however, native identity management capabilities remain limited. Polygon, as an Ethereum-compatible Layer-2 solution, demonstrates significant scalability, cost-efficiency, and flexibility, positioning it favorably for large-scale DDI systems. To achieve regulatory compliance alongside scalability, this study recommends leveraging **Polygon's Layer-2 architecture, adapting it into a private permissioned model**, and incorporating privacy-preserving technologies, including **ZKP, VC, DID and selective disclosure**. Despite the potential governance complexities and challenges associated with adapting a permissionless blockchain to a permissioned environment, this approach aligns with GDPR and eIDAS 2.0, offering a balanced solution.

4 Experimental Setup and Results

The experiment validating the Polygon ID issuer node was conducted using a Windows 10 machine running Ubuntu 22.04 via WSL2. The official Polygon ID issuer node repository was cloned from GitHub and deployed within a Dockerized infrastructure to simulate the full identity issuance lifecycle on the Polygon Amoy testnet. Necessary dependencies included Docker, Docker Compose, Node.js, npm, snarkjs, and circom, all configured for compatibility. A valid Alchemy RPC URL and wallet private key were securely configured through the `issuer-private-key.txt` and related environment files (`.env-issuer`, `resolvers_settings.yaml`) adapted from provided templates.

The issuer environment was initialized and built with the command:

```
sudo docker-compose -f docker-compose-full.yml up -d -
build
```

System readiness and component health were verified by inspecting container statuses (`docker ps`) and API responses (`curl` http://localhost:3001/status). Ten credentials were then issued via the local UI. Log timestamps showed a median end-to-end latency of 1.9 s (min = 1.7 s, max = 2.3 s) and a 90% success rate (9/10). Redis was queried to inspect identity states:

```
sudo docker exec -it local-redis-1 redis-cli
127.0.0.1:6379> keys *
```

The key that appears during issuance expires after the default 60-second TTL, explaining the "empty" result. Oncreasing TTL or enabling persistence is planned for follow-up tests. Nonetheless, the test scenario sufficiently demonstrated the system's complete operational workflow. Key results are summarized in Table 4.

Table 4. Experimental results

Component	Status	Description
API Service	Healthy	Successfully built and served migration routines
Vault	Healthy	Initialized and unsealed; used in localstorage mode
Redis	Healthy	Responded to queries; key expired after default TTL
Postgres	Healthy	Responded to migrations and stored platform schema
UI Service	Healthy	Accessible on localhost; used for identity issuance
Issuer Node Logs	Normal	Showed successful key provider setup, but repeated Ethereum connection errors
Identity Publishing	90% success	UI issued 9/10 credentials, one RPC timeout

The results confirm the feasibility of deploying and testing a Polygon-based DDI system in a local Docker environment, showcasing the platform's practical suitability for decentralized identity implementations despite minor internal synchronization challenges. The test was intentionally small-scale. Future work will include load-testing ($\geq$1 000 issuances) and revocation/selective-disclosure flows to validate GDPR and eIDAS compliance under production-like conditions.

5 Conclusions and Future Work

This study evaluated blockchain platforms for DDI, considering regulatory frameworks, existing solutions, and technical architectures. Polygon emerged as the most suitable option due to its scalability, interoperability, and cost-efficiency. To achieve regulatory compliance, it is recommended to adapt Polygon into a private permissioned blockchain integrating ZKP, VC, DID, and selective disclosure, balancing transparency with privacy and security.

The study confirms both hypotheses: blockchain technology effectively addresses security, privacy, and interoperability within regulatory standards (H1), and permissionless blockchains can support compliant DDI systems if adapted with appropriate governance and privacy mechanisms (H2). The experimental validation was intentionally small-scale and therefore does not yet cover high-load performance or full revocation workflows.

Future research should implement and rigorously evaluate this adapted Polygon model in practical scenarios, focusing on its real-world scalability, security, and compliance. Additionally, technical and governance challenges of integrating permissioned adaptations of Polygon into existing digital identity frameworks warrant further exploration.

Disclosure of Interests. The publication was prepared during the implementation of the project "Implementation of R&D activities, creating APV products by Deverium, UAB" (Project No. 02-020-K-0034). The project is co-financed by the European Union. Findings, conclusions or recommendations expressed in this material are those of the authors and do not necessarily reflect the views of Deverium, UAB.

References

1. Zulkifli, F., et al.: National digital identity: current landscape, emerging technologies and future directions. Int. J. Acad. Res. Bus. Soc. Sci. **13**(3), 1225–1242 (2023)
2. Goodell, G., Aste, T.: A decentralised digital identity architecture. https://doi.org/10.48550/arxiv.1902.08769 (2019)
3. World Economic Forum: Blockchain can help create privacy-preserving digital ID. https://www.weforum.org/agenda/2023/03/blockchain-privacy-preserving-digital-id/. Accessed 29 Jan 2025
4. Ahmed, M.R., Islam, A.K.M.M., Shatabda, S., Islam, S.: Blockchain-based identity management system and self-sovereign identity ecosystem: a comprehensive survey. IEEE Access **10**, 113436–113481 (2022)

5. Ozdenizci Kose, B., Coskun, V., Coskun, A., Yaya, S.: A blockchain-enhanced self-sovereign identity platform for corporate resource security. Adv. Cyber Phys. Syst. **8**(2), 111–117 (2023)
6. Mole, C., Chalstrey, E., Foster, P., Hobson, T.: Digital identity architectures: comparing goals and vulnerabilities. https://doi.org/10.48550/arxiv.2302.09988 (2023)
7. Mazzocca, C., Acar, A., Uluagac, S., Montanari, R., Bellavista, P., Conti, M.: A survey on decentralized identifiers and verifiable credentials. https://doi.org/10.48550/arxiv.2402.02455 (2024)
8. Bakos, Y., Halaburda, H.: Permissioned vs permissionless blockchain platforms: tradeoffs in trust and performance. NYU Stern School of Business working paper (2021). https://doi.org/10.2139/ssrn.3789425
9. Mohamadi Begum, Y., Ravi Prakash, B.: An efficient and scalable framework for decentralized finance application using blockchain interoperability. J. Electr. Syst. **20**(1s), 712–727 (2024)
10. Butijn, B., Tamburri, D.A., Heuvel, W.V.D.: Blockchains: a systematic multivocal literature review. https://doi.org/10.48550/arxiv.1911.11770 (2019)
11. Thakur, A., Ranga, V., Agarwal, R.: Workload dynamics implications in permissioned blockchain scalability and performance. Clust. Comput. **27**, 11569–11593 (2024). https://doi.org/10.1007/s10586-024-04550-z
12. Sempere, C.: The legal framework for new digital assets, identities, and data spaces. Introduction (2025). https://doi.org/10.1007/978-3-031-74889-9_1
13. European Commission: European Digital Identity (EUDI). European Commission (2024). https://ec.europa.eu/digital-strategy/our-policies/european-digital-identity_en. Accessed 27 Jan 2025
14. Dock: eIDAS 2.0: A beginner's guide (2025). https://www.dock.io/post/eidas-2. Accessed 27 Jan 2025
15. Butincu, C.N., Alexandrescu, A.: Design aspects of decentralized identifiers and self-sovereign identity systems. IEEE Access **12**, 60928–60942 (2024). https://doi.org/10.1109/ACCESS.2024.3394537
16. Regulation (EU) 2016/679 of the European Parliament and of the Council of 27 April 2016 on the protection of natural persons with regard to the processing of personal data and on the free movement of such data, and repealing Directive 95/46/EC (General Data Protection Regulation)
17. Regulation (EU) 2024/1183 of the European Parliament and of the Council of 11 April 2024 amending Regulation (EU) No 910/2014 as regards establishing the European digital identity framework
18. Amiri, M.J., Agrawal, D., El Abbadi, A.: Permissioned blockchains: properties, techniques and applications. In: Proceedings of the 2021 International Conference on Management of Data, Virtual Event, China, pp. 2813–2820. ACM (2021)
19. Lavin, R., Liu, X., Mohanty, H., Norman, L., Zaarour, G., Krishnamachari, B.: A survey on the applications of zero-knowledge proofs (2024). https://arxiv.org/abs/2408.00243. Accessed 27 Jan 2025
20. W3C: Decentralized identifiers (DID) v1.0 – core architecture, data model, and repre-sentations. W3C Recommendation, 19 July 2022. https://www.w3.org/TR/did-core/. Accessed 27 Jan 2025
21. W3C: Verifiable credentials data model v1.1. W3C Recommendation, 3 March 2022. https://www.w3.org/TR/vc-data-model/. Accessed 27 Jan 2025
22. Synaps: Synaps launches novel decentralized identity solution Anima Protocol in partnership with Aleph.im. https://www.globenewswire.com/news-release/2022/04/12/2421095/0/en/Synaps-Launches-Novel-Decentralized-Identity-Solution-Anima-Protocol-In-Partnership-with-Aleph-im.html. Accessed 23 Apr 2024

23. Gemini Cryptopedia: Civic identity (CVC): digital identity solutions for Web3. https://www.gemini.com/cryptopedia/civic-identity-cvc-crypto-civic-crypto-cvc-token. Accessed 23 Apr 2024
24. Blockpass: Know Your Customer (KYC) solutions. https://www.blockpass.org/kyc/. Accessed 23 Apr 2024
25. Quadrata: Web3 identity passport network. https://quadrata.com/. Accessed 23 Apr 2024
26. Business Wire: Quadrata partners with Polygon to integrate Web3 passport network. https://www.businesswire.com/news/home/20220929005144/en/Quadrata-Partners-with-Polygon-to-Integrate-Web3-Passport-Network. Accessed 23 Apr 2024
27. Fractal ID: Decentralized identity verification platform. https://web.fractal.id/. Accessed 23 Apr 2024
28. CoinDesk: Crypto compliance platform Keyring raises $6M to unlock DeFi for institutional investors. https://www.coindesk.com/business/2024/03/19/crypto-compliance-platform-keyring-raises-6m-to-unlock-defi-for-institutional-investors. Accessed 23 Apr 2024
29. HashKey DID: HashKey DID introduces rDNS powered by the ATON wallet. https://medium.com/@HashKeyDID/hashkey-did-introduces-rdns-powered-by-the-aton-wallet-c3c640795f83. Accessed 23 Apr 2024
30. Holonym: Redefining KYC. https://medium.com/holonym/redefining-kyc-bb86071b6f60. Accessed 23 Apr 2024
31. Privado ID: Polygon ID integrates Verite decentralized identity solution. https://www.privado.id/blog/polygon-id-integrates-verite-decentralized-identity-solution. Accessed 23 Apr 2024
32. GlobeNewswire: Buenos Aires sets global precedent by empowering 3.6 million citizens with blockchain-based digital identity on miBA platform. https://www.globenewswire.com/news-release/2024/10/22/2967256/0/en/Buenos-Aires-Sets-Global-Precedent-by-Empowering-3-6-Million-Citizens-with-Blockchain-based-Digital-Identity-on-miBA-platform.html. Accessed 23 Apr 2024
33. The Paypers: Bhutan's national SSI transitions to the Polygon blockchain. https://thepaypers.com/digital-identity-security-online-fraud/bhutans-national-ssi-transitions-to-the-polygon-blockchain--1269595. Accessed 23 Apr 2024
34. DSR Corporation: BC Gov and W3C verifiable credentials project. https://en.dsr-corporation.com/news/bcgovw3c. Accessed 23 Apr 2024
35. Procivis: Der neue Gesetzesentwurf zur E-ID in der Schweiz. https://www.procivis.ch/en/insights/der-neue-gesetzesentwurf-zur-e-id-in-der-schweiz. Accessed 23 Apr 2024
36. Privacy by Design Foundation: IRMA – Privacy-friendly identity management. https://privacybydesign.foundation/irma-explanation/. Accessed 23 Apr 2024
37. Luque, S., Rivera, V., Huarcaya, N.: Cryptocurrency payment system model for B2C e-commerce platforms using blockchain technology. In: 2023 International Conference on Electrical, Computer and Energy Technologies (ICECET), pp. 1–6 (2023). https://doi.org/10.1109/ICECET58911.2023.10389441
38. Pflanzner, T., Baniata, H., Kertész, A.: Latency analysis of blockchain-based SSI applications. Future Internet **14**, 282 (2022). https://doi.org/10.3390/fi14100282
39. Androulaki, E., et al.: Hyperledger fabric: a distributed operating system for permissioned blockchains. In: Proceedings of the Thirteenth EuroSys Conference (2018). https://doi.org/10.1145/3190508.3190538
40. Shcherbakov, A.: Hyperledger Indy Besu as a permissioned ledger in self-sovereign identity. In: Open Identity Summit 2024, Porto, Portugal, 20–21 June 2024, pp. 127–137. Gesellschaft für Informatik e.V., Bonn (2024). https://doi.org/10.18420/OID2024_11. P-ISSN: 1617-5468, ISBN: 978-3-88579-744-9
41. Terzi, S., Kouzinopoulos, C., Votis, K., Tzovaras, D., Stamelos, I.: Securing emission data of smart vehicles with blockchain and self-sovereign identities. In: 2020 IEEE International

Conference on Blockchain (Blockchain), pp. 462–469 (2020). https://doi.org/10.1109/Blockchain50366.2020.00067
42. Melo, C., Araujo, J., Dantas, J., Pereira, P., Maciel, P.: A model-based approach for planning blockchain service provisioning. Computing **104**, 315–337 (2021). https://doi.org/10.1007/s00607-021-00956-4
43. Polygonscan: Average transaction fee (USD). Polygonscan (2025). https://polygonscan.com/chart/avg-txfee-usd. Accessed 27 Jan 2025
44. Ethereum Foundation (2021). Ethereum 2.0 Specifications. https://ethereum.org/en/eth2/
45. Dunphy, P.: A note on the blockchain trilemma for decentralized identity: learning from experiments with Hyperledger Indy (2022). https://doi.org/10.48550/arXiv.2204.05784
46. Paul, A.: Assessing the environmental sustainability of Polygon's consensus mechanism and transaction processing, comparing its energy consumption and carbon footprint with other layer 2 and layer 1 blockchain solutions, and exploring potential avenues for further optimization. Int. J. Res. Appl. Sci. Eng. Technol. (2023). https://doi.org/10.22214/ijraset.2023.53900
47. Toktar, R.: Hyperledger Indy on Besu Joins the did:indy Method – Six Months of Progress. LF Decentralized Trust Blog (2025). https://www.lfdecentralizedtrust.org/blog/lf-decentralized-trusts-hyperledger-indy-on-besu-joins-the-didindy-method-six-months-of-progress
48. Ethereum Foundation: Sharding FAQ – How many transactions per second will sharding provide? ethereum.org (2024). https://ethereum.org/en/upgrades/sharding/#how-many-transactions-per-second-will-sharding-provide

A Decision Support Tool Towards Detecting Competition Law Infringements

Georgia Kaoura(✉) and Basilis Boutsinas

Management Information Systems and Business Intelligence Lab, Department of Business Administration, University of Patras, University Campus, 26504 Rio, Achaia, Greece
gkaoura@upatras.gr

Abstract. Artificial Intelligence (AI) has become an indispensable component of contemporary human life, integrated into numerous daily utilized applications. This research proposes an innovative methodology in the enforcement of competition law and policy, underscoring the pivotal role of AI in addressing field-related challenges. The goal of this paper is to present a Decision Support Tool in Competition Law and policy (Comp-DST) based on the application of a hybrid reasoner combining rule-based reasoning (RBR) and case-based reasoning (CBR). Through a comprehensive, multi-layered approach the proposed Comp-DST systematically structures and leverages competition-specific knowledge. Hence, the Tool is designed to facilitate competition experts in case analysis and investigation, strengthen their capacity building and enhance their reliability and effectiveness.

Keywords: RBR · CBR · Hybrid Reasoning Systems · Competition Law

1 Introduction

AI-driven technologies are almost omnipresent. Decision Support Tools based on AI reasoning systems provide practical support for 'real-life' decisions about a variety of tasks.

In this paper, we study the application of a hybrid reasoner to the enforcement of competition law and policy. A hybrid reasoner infers implicitly stated knowledge by reasoning upon explicitly stated knowledge. The proposed Decision Support Tool (Comp-DST) aims at supporting competition experts in analysis and investigation for competition law enforcement, based on a set of rules and previous cases stored in its knowledge base. This framework is presented in [1] as a hybrid reasoner integrating both Rule-Based Reasoning (RBR) and Case-Based Reasoning (CBR) approaches. To our knowledge, competition domain is an area where previous efforts have been made to support the operations of competition authorities [2] and to develop AI-based investigative tools for detecting breaches of competition law [3], however a similar approach as the one proposed in the paper has not been yet explored.

The proposed tool is tested based on domain-specific knowledge built in the Hellenic Competition Commission ("HCC" or Commission) and uploaded on the Authority's website. In particular, we constructed a dataset of 70 HCC antitrust decisions for the years

K. Węcel (Ed.): BIS 2025 Workshops, LNBIP 568, pp. 53–63, 2026.
https://doi.org/10.1007/978-3-032-11651-2_5

1996–2019. Each specific case is analysed and represented by thirty-eight (38) attributes, grouped into four main categories, used to describe several case dimensions related to case-management, decision-making, market (relevant market, structure, conditions etc.) and administrative processes. A separate group of case-attributes concerns some of the steps identified and taken place during the investigation phase (initial assessment, investigation measures etc.), considered as a process.

The HCC is the independent administrative authority competent for the enforcement of Greek law concerning the protection of free competition. The HCC mandates at maintaining and restoring a healthy competitive market structure. Its mission includes the suppression of anti-competitive practices and the prevention of abusive exploitation of dominant position by businesses [4].

Therefore, the challenge in developing such a tool and support HCC decision-making stems from the need to make fair decisions that are consistent with its previous judgments, accurate, and well-informed so that when they are challenged in courts to be upheld [5].

The proposed approach is based on a hybrid reasoner, combining rule-based reasoning (RBR), case-based reasoning (CBR) to facilitate case investigation in competition law enforcement. Combining Rule-based reasoning and Case-based reasoning has been widely used, exhibiting quite successful results, since it takes advantage of the positive aspects of both while minimizing their negative ones. The tool can also be linked to a Process mining (PM) module, in order to predict, based on specific case attributes, the outcome of the decision (infringement based on cases attributes and steps of the administrative procedures applied). For instance, to predict which decisions may be challenged in court.

In the rest of the paper, we first briefly present HCC and the need to develop a decision support tool (Sect. 2), which is described in Sect. 3. Finally, we conclude (Sect. 4).

2 Domain Description

The HCC is the competent authority for the enforcement of Greek Law 3959/2011[1], "Protection of Free Competition", [6], as well as of Art. 101 and 102 of the Treaty on the Functioning of the European Union (TFEU) [7].

In 2011, Law 3959 introduced provisions to streamline the handling of complaints, allowing the prioritization of cases that meet specific criteria set by the authority. These criteria consider factors such as "the public interest, the potential impact on competition, consumer protection, the newly established prescription period, and the anticipated effect of the authority's intervention." [8].

Decisions of the HCC are subject to judicial review through a two-tier process. The Athens Administrative Court of Appeals, acting as a first-instance court, conducts a comprehensive review of both substantive and procedural aspects within sixty days of notification and holds the authority to uphold, annul or modify the decision, including reducing fines. Judgments of this court may be further challenged before the Council of State (Supreme Administrative Court, State Council), which functions as a second and final-instance court, limited to a legality review. No further appellate recourse is available, ensuring a structured and finite judicial oversight mechanism.

[1] Previous Law 703/1977.

The principal challenge in decision-making stems from the necessity of taking decisions that are optimized in terms of effectiveness or efficiency. However, in numerous fields, existing data and previously implemented solutions remain underutilized, lacking systematic integration for future problem-solving processes [9]. Although Competition Authorities (CAs) publish their decisions on their websites, a limited number of metadata are uploaded to facilitate analysis for the users (competition lawyers, economists, social scientists, data scientists etc.). In addition, not an integrated customized case management information system is utilized internally, and case handlers are usually facing the challenge where previous case files lack systematic organization or integration in order to be easily and efficiently utilized in future cases.

Competition law is a domain where a certain number of general rules may apply while in parallel extended special knowledge may derive from previous cases. Infringements identified derive from the rules as governing in Art.1 and 2 of national legislative framework (Art.101 and 102 TFEU) however case law have contributed significantly to the interpretation, clarification, and practical application of these rules. Case law has provided insights into the complex dynamics of competition law, shaping and elaborating further the understanding of key concepts such as market definition, abuse of dominance, and anti-competitive agreements. Judicial precedent and decisions have played a critical role in adapting the general rules to the specificities of individual cases, ensuring that competition law remains responsive to evolving market realities and emerging economic behaviors.

3 The Proposed Decision Support Tool

The proposed Decision Support Tool (Comp-DST) is conceptualized as a hybrid reasoner, i.e., a knowledge-based intelligent information system designed to facilitate the processing, and analysis of competition decisions. These decisions are encoded and systematically stored within its Knowledge Base to provide actionable insights and recommendations to users. Comp-DST aims at enabling users to efficiently manage and resolve competition-related cases. By offering expert-level guidance, Comp-DST aims to enhance the overall effectiveness of decision-making processes in competition law enforcement.

The users of the Comp-DST include competition law and policy experts, public authorities, and regulatory stakeholders. The Knowledge Base forms the core of the Comp-DST and comprises both domain-specific and general information. The tool processes user-provided attributes of past cases or practices. Based on the input, the system dynamically generates responses derived from pre-defined rules and/or case precedents relevant to the input description. The tool retrieves and adapts similar cases/decisions handled and stored in the Knowledge Base to address the user's current situation.

Users assess the proposed solutions, through posing queries to the Comp-DST. Such a query actually describes a certain new case of competition law infringements. This new case, after possible modifications imposed by the adaptation of the similar cases/decisions suggested by the Comp-DST, is stored as a new entry enriching the Knowledge Base over time.

To detect similar cases/decisions Comp-DST is based on a hybrid reasoner, combining rule-based reasoning (RBR) and case-based reasoning (CBR), which are presented in the following subsections.

3.1 The Hybrid Reasoner of Decision Support Tool

The Comp-DST employs a hybrid reasoning framework to recommend relevant prior cases to users. This framework described in [1] is a hybrid reasoner that integrates both Rule-Based Reasoning (RBR) and Case-Based Reasoning (CBR). The combination of RBR and CBR has been extensively utilized across various domains, yielding highly effective results [10].

The integration of RBR and CBR enables the DST to complement strengths of both reasoning approaches, RBR for providing structured, generalizable knowledge applicable to well-defined problems and CBR for enhancing flexibility by leveraging knowledge from past experiences to address new or complex situations.

By synthesizing these methodologies, the hybrid reasoner ensures robust, adaptive decision support for users, accommodating both explicit rules and experiential knowledge in its recommendations. This approach aligns with prior research highlighting the potential of combining RBR and CBR [10], making it well-suited for complex decision-making environments.

Case-Based Reasoning (CBR)

CBR, utilizes previously stored cases to resolve new, relevant cases. It follows the **CBR cycle**, a systematic reasoning process comprising four key phases: Retrieve, Reuse, Revise and Retain [11]. If deemed useful, the new case is added to the case repository for subsequent reference. The Case Based reasoner is the main component of Comp-DST. Given an input, after it is enhanced by the RBR layer (see next subparagraph), the CBR layer detects the most relevant cases from the stored ones in the Case Base. The stored cases represent previous cases handled by the Hellenic Competition Authority, resulted to decisions regarding the competition law enforcement.

In the current version of Comp-DST, the Case Base (CB) is populated with 70 cases, concerning decisions on several anti-competitive practices, directly inserted in CB. A publicly available github folder (https://github.com/vutsinas/Comp-DST.git) has been created including an Excel file with the set of cases of the Case Base of Comp-DST.

Given the extensive set of attributes characterizing each case and the presence of multiple parallel and sequential relationships within each case, calculating a representative **overall similarity measure** between two cases posed a significant challenge. This process required meticulous fine-tuning to ensure optimal performance and accurate results.

To derive a comprehensive similarity measure between two cases, the proposed tool takes into account the majority of their attributes and the method employed for calculating similarity is tailored to the specific type and nature of each attribute.

Each specific *case* is represented by thirty-eight (38) attributes organized into four groups: *Market data, Case data, Decision data, Administrative Procedures data.*

For categorical attributes, Comp-DST uses the Eskin similarity [12] between two categorical values. There are also few numerical attributes related to the years of the completion of investigation, the years of infringement and the amount of fine based on the decision taken (when it is possible to be exported). For numerical attributes, Comp-DST uses the normalized distance between two values of numerical attributes [13]. There are also case-attributes whose values form an ontology. For each such an ontological attribute, there is a corresponding ontology that represents the terms used as its values. Ontology over an attribute ci is a directed acyclic tree $Tc_i = (N, E)$, where N is the set of nodes and E is the set of edges such that every $e_i \in E$ is an ordered pair (n_k, n_l), and n_k, nl $\in$ N. Every node $n_i \in N$ represents a possible attribute value. For these ontological attributes, similarity is obtained based on the distance of the terms in the Ontology. More specifically, Comp-DST uses a function of node distance within a tree-structure [14], between two values of attributes that are represented by nodes of a given ontology:

$$1-d\left(c_{ik}, c_{jk}\right), \text{ where}$$

$$d\left(c_{ik}, c_{jk}\right) = \frac{1}{fl\left(c_{ik}, c_{jk}\right)} \times Average\left(\frac{l(c_{ik}) - fl\left(c_{ik}, c_{jk}\right)}{max(p(c_{ik}))}, \frac{l\left(c_{jk}\right) - fl\left(c_{ik}, C_{jk}\right)}{\max\left(p\left(c_{jk}\right)\right)}\right)$$
$$\times \left(\frac{p\left(c_{ik}, c_{jk}\right)}{\max(p(c_{ik})) + \max\left(p\left(c_{jk}\right)\right)}\right)$$

where c_{ik} and c_{jk} represent two nodes in the ontology, $fl(c_{ik}, c_{jk})$ is the level of the nearest common father node of them, $l(c_{ik})$ is the level of node c_{ik}, $\max(p(c_{ik}))$ is the length of the maximum path starting from the root to a leaf and containing node c_{ik} and $p(c_{ik}, c_{jk})$ is the length of the directed path (number of edges) connecting c_{ik} and c_{jk}.

There are also Boolean case-attributes. For Boolean attributes, Comp-DST set similarity to1 if the attribute values are the same or to 0 otherwise. Finally, there is a multivalued attribute: the one referring to practices investigated and included in decisions under horizontal or/and vertical agreements that may accept up to three values to describe the articles under which the investigated practices are fallen, i.e. practices categorised under article 1 and article 2 infringements. For the *multivalued attribute*, Comp-DST uses the *Jaccard similarity* [15] between two values of multivalued attributes:

$$\text{Sim\_multi}\left(c_{ik}, c_{jk}\right) = 1 - \frac{A \cap B}{A \cup B}$$

where $A = \{c_{ikq} \mid c_{ikq} \in c_{ik} \text{ and } c_{ikq} \in \text{domain}(k)\}$ and $B = \{c_{jkq} \mid c_{jkq} \in c_{jk} \text{ and } c_{jkq} \in \text{domain}(k)\}$.

Finally, after calculating similarity for each one of the 38 attributes, the weighted average is used to calculate the overall similarity: for each attribute a there is a corresponding weight representing its importance. The weights were determined, in order to optimize the result, thus for two cases i, j:

$$\text{Overall Similarity(i, j)} = \sum\nolimits_{a=1}^{n} (SIMILARITY_{ij} \times WEIGHT_a)$$

To calculate the Overall Similarity (i, j), we consider equal weight for each attribute similarity a ($e.g.$, $WEIGHT_a = 1$).

Thus, the CBR Layer will match the enhanced input to the most similar previous cases in the Case Base and produce revised solutions for each problem, which will then feed the final PM layer of the hybrid system.

Rule-Based Reasoning (RBR)

RBR operates on a structured set of rules, collectively referred to as the Rule Base, which encapsulates general domain knowledge. Each rule is typically formulated in an "if-then" structure. The reasoning process involves introducing inputs to the rule base, thereby triggering a sequence of rule activations. This inference mechanism enables RBR to produce outputs through a logical progression of rules [16]. RBR is particularly effective in domains with a well-defined conceptual model or where domain experts can formally codify knowledge as rules.

The Rule Base of Comp-DST comprises "If-Then" rules. In competition domain certain general rules explaining the incompatibility with internal market (infringements) are provided for the legislation (articles 101 and 102 of TFEU, articles 1 and 2 L.3959/2011). However, there are a few such rules extracted by experts after manually processing the legislation. More specifically, 12 such rules are included in the Rule Base of Comp-DST. As an example, two of them, regarding article 2, are:

- IF one or more dominant undertakings directly or indirectly impose unfair purchase or selling prices or other unfair trading conditions THEN infringement of abuse of dominant position.
- IF undertakings have large Market Shares for many years THEN undertakings with dominant position.

In general, individuals with both domain expertise and the necessary skills to construct domain dependent "If-Then" rules are extremely rare. As a result, the development of Rule-based Expert Systems faces a significant challenge known as the Knowledge Acquisition Bottleneck, a fundamental challenge arising from the limited availability of experts capable of encoding domain knowledge into rule-based frameworks [17, 18].

Thus, lately, the new trend is to let the system 'discover' the rules by crunching as much data as possible and by applying powerful machine learning techniques [19].

The Rule Base of Comp-DST consists of 23 rules established by applying Association Rule Mining to its Case Base. These were selected after experts reviewed an initial set of 40 extracted rules. More specifically, the Apriori algorithm is applied to an input database consisting of the fields included in the Case Base of Comp-DST.

Association Rule Mining was preferred over Classification, since we aimed to extract as many general rules as possible concerning all the input fields. Classification is asymmetric with respect to attributes, since in classification we aim at predicting the value (class) of a special, user-defined goal attribute based on the values of all the other (predictor) attributes. By contrast, Association Rule Mining is symmetric with respect to attributes, since no attribute is given special treatment, i.e., any attribute can occur either in the rule antecedent or in the rule consequent [20].

More specifically, the set of association rules is extracted by setting minimum support to 30% and minimum confidence to 90%, since there are only a few cases, while the domain of most case-attributes is large. For instance, such indicative rules are:

- **IF** Case Category = Complaint and Decision_Making = Unanimity **THEN** there is homogeneity in the Market
- **IF** GeographicalMarket = Greece and Homogeneity_Market = YES **THEN** CasesInfluencingEurCooperation = NO

A publicly available github folder (https://github.com/vutsinas/Comp-DST.git) has been created including an Excel file with the set of rules of the Rule Base of Comp-DST.

3.2 The Functionality of Comp-DST

The proposed Comp-DST is a knowledge-based intelligent information system. Its accuracy is dominated by the adequacy of its Knowledge Base, since the latter has embedded experts' knowledge as an internal representation of the characteristics of past competition law cases. Those characteristics will be compared to the characteristics of the problem at hand. Given the large amount of different attributes that may represent a case, the comparison between two different scenarios to calculate a representative overall similarity, will be one challenging and complicated part of the Comp-DST.

To calculate the Overall Similarity(i, j) in the current version of Comp-DST, we consider equal weight for each attribute similarity a ($WEIGHT_a = 1$).

The input includes the initial facts for the inference system, entered by the user. The RBR layer gives enhanced input to the CBR layer.

In a more formal way, let FS be the set of given (initial) facts, provided by the user: f1, …, fn ∈ FS. Then a subset TRB of RB, the rule base of the RBR component, are triggered: r1, …, rm ∈ TRB ⊆ RB. Those rules represent general knowledge provided by domain experts or discovered by machine learning techniques. The triggered rules produce a set AFS of additional facts (i.e., the produced consequents of r1, …, rm): af1, …, afm ∈ AFS, that further describe/enhance the input. The enhanced input set EFS = FS ∪ AFS, which is derived during this first step, is then used as input to the CBR layer that retrieves from CB = {ci | ci = (ci1, … cip)}, the case base of CBR layer, a set RCB of the most relevant stored cases: c1, …, ct ∈ RCB ⊆ CB. The latter cases form the output of Comp-DST.

An Example of Applying Comp-DST

The functionality of Comp-DST is based on responses to queries posed by users through a specially designed form to pose queries, i.e., input problems concerning competition cases. In order to evaluate the proposed tool, a standalone experimental application is developed which is freely available through the link: https://aigroup.ceid.upatras.gr/hybrid.

In the following, we demonstrate the use of Comp-DST by an example. We consider four of the cases stored in the CBR component of the Comp-DST. To simplify the example, we represent the cases using only the attributes, shown in Table 1, since there is a large number of attributes needed to represent a case in the system.

The field "Legislative Clause-Anticompetitive practice investigated" (LegislativeClause-InvestigatedACpractice) is an ontological attribute, i.e., its values form an ontology which is depicted horizontally in the following:

1. Root - LegislativeClause-ACpracticeInvestigated

Table 1. Selected attributes

Attribute	Type	Weight
Homogeneity	Boolean	0.2
Geographical Market	Categorical	0.2
InvestigatedEntitySize	Categorical	0.2
LegislativeClause-InvestigatedACpractice	Values from ontology	0.2
Decision-ThreatForFine	Boolean	0.2

2. Article1_101
   3. HorizontalAgreements
      4. Bid-rigging, CollusiveTendering, Cooperation_Agreements
         5. CommonCommerce, CommonProduction, CommonPuchases, Other Forms, RandD, Standardization
      4. Crisis_cartel, InformationSharing, MarketSharing, PriceFixing Restriction-sOnOutput, WithdrawalOfBlockExemption
   3. VerticalAgreements
      4. BanOfParallelImports, ExclusiveDistribution, ExclusivePurchContracts, Franchise, GeographicalRestrictions, NonCompetitionClause, Other Re str., Representation, RPM, SelectiveDistribution, With drawal of BEV
2. Article2_102
   3. BanOfParallelImports_102, CrossSubsidy, ExcessivePricing, Exclus_Clauses, ImposingUnfairTradingConditions, MarginSqueeze, OtherPractices, Predatory Pricing, PriceDicsrimination, Rebates, RefusalToAccess, RefusalToSupply, RefusalToSupplyAndIPR, TyingAndBundling, UnfairlyHighorLowPricing

Note, that each case corresponds to a description of a previous resolved case concerning certain attributes included in the database. The "Homogeneity", "Geographical Market" and "InvestigatedEntitySize" attributes refer to the individual case that would be drawn from the cases database. The attributes "LegislativeClause-InvestigatedACpractice" and "Decision-ThreatForFine" describe the decision/solution.

Thus, suppose that the Case Base consists of the following cases (Table 2):

Table 2. Simplified Cases

Case Id	Homogeneity	Geographical Market	Investigated EntitySize	CasesInfluencing EurCooperation	Legislative clause ACpractice	Decision-ThreatForFine
38/1996	YES	GR	Big	NO	RefusalToSupply	YES
207/III/2002	YES	GR	Big	NO	TyingAndBundling	YES
245/III/2003	YES	GR	Big	NO	UnfairlyHighOrLowPricing	YES
389/V/2008	YES	GR	Big	NO	ImposingUnfairTradingConditions	YES

Then, suppose that the user inputs a query, i.e., a case represented using the selected attributes shown in Table 1. We consider the following input:

Case Category = "Complaint", Geographical Market = "Greece", Homogeneity in the market = "YES", LegislativeClause-AC practice = "UnfairlyHighorLowPrices", ThreatForFine = "YES"

The first step of the inference procedure is to run the RBR component, using the entire Rule Base of Comp-DST, (see Sect. 3.2). The conditions of the following rule R10 are met:

IF GeographicalMarket= Greece AND Homogeneity_Market = YES **THEN** CasesInfluencingEurCooperation = NO

Therefore, the rule is triggered, and the input is extended with the new fact:

CasesInfluencingEurCooperation = NO

Then, the CBR component is executed, and it compares the input against all the cases shown in Cases-Database. The case with the highest match is case 245/III/2003. The similarity is estimated using the corresponding similarities for the five attributes: For "Homogeneity", "Geographical Market" and "InvestigatedEntitySize", since cases have the same values as the input, we assume a similarity value of one. For "LegislativeClause-AC practice" we calculate the similarity based on the corresponding ontology (see above). For instance, for the nodes:

(LegislativeClause-ACpracticeInvestigated → Article2_102 → UnfairlyHighOrLowPricing) and (LegislativeClause-ACpractice Investigated → Article2_102 → RefusalToSupply) of case id 38/1996, the similarity is calculated as: $1 - [(1/2) \times \text{avg}((3-2)/2, (3-2)/2) \times (2/(2+2))] = 0.833$, since i) the nearest common father node is in level 2, ii) the length of the maximum path from root to leaf that contains each node is 3, iii) the length of the directed path connecting the two nodes is 2. Finally, we combine the individual similarity values using the assigned weights as shown above, thus we calculate the final similarity value as $(0.2 \times 1.0) + (0.2 \times 1.0) + (0.2 \times 1.0) + (0.2 \times 1.0) + (0.2 \times 0.833) = 0.967$. Obviously, the similarity with cases 207/III/2002 and 389/V/2008 is also 0.967.

Comparing the user's input with case id 245/III/2003, it is obvious that they share the same values for all attributes. For the intervention field, the similarity is calculated as: $1 - [(1/2) \times \text{avg}((3-2)/2, (3-2)/2) \times (0/(2+2))] = 1$, since i) the nearest common father node is in level 2, ii) the length of the maximum path from root to leaf that contains each node is 3, iii) the length of the directed path connecting the two nodes is 0. Thus, we calculate the final similarity value (by using equal weights) as $(0.2 \times 1.0) + (0.2 \times 1.0) + (0.2 \times 1.0) + (0.2 \times 1.0) + (0.2 \times 1) = 1$.

Thus, the output of the Comp-DST includes the case 245/III/2003. The system identified and retrieved the most relevant case matching the user's query, providing extended and more detailed information about case's element, relevant case law etc. This information will serve as a resource assisting the user in making well-informed decisions regarding the investigation based on relevant precedents, contextual insights, and supporting data.

To evaluate the output of Comp-DST against the exploitation of a LLM, we form the input case as text which was fed to ChatGPT. More specifically, the query is: "*Search for competition-related cases between 1996–2019 that examine the anticompetitive practice of imposing unreasonable prices (excessively low or high prices) within the Greek territory by large firm or associations of firms in markets with homogeneous conditions and threatened with a fine. We are interested in cases where a competition law infringement has been identified and a fine has been imposed.*". The output consists of references to 6 cases *(from search in both English and Greek)* related to HCC (the output text is available in the github folder (https://github.com/vutsinas/Comp-DST.git). This output doesn't match the results of Comp-DST. Instead, it includes six (6) competition cases, out of which three (3) were correctly related to the same infringement article (art.2 of Law 3959/2011). However, these three cases are not related to the same anti-competitive practice/situation.

4 Conclusion – Future Work

This paper introduces Comp-DST, a Decision Support Tool specifically designed for competition law practitioners, representing, to the best of our knowledge, the first tool of its kind to utilize a hybrid reasoning framework to support decision-making processes in competition law and policy. The hybrid reasoning framework employed is particularly effective in domains characterized by a combination of a limited set of general rules and extensive specialized knowledge extracted by past cases. A prototype of the Decision Support Tool has been developed, encompassing a knowledge base comprising 70 cases and 23 rules, demonstrating the practical applicability and scalability of the proposed approach.

One of the limitations of the present study lies in the small number of cases consisting the Case Base of Comp-DST. As the cases are enriched, more and more data and evidence will be identified in the analysis and the relationships between conditions and practices will become more stable. Another limitation is the automatic derivation of rules as opposed to rule mining by experts, since the latter are usually able to incorporate into the rules also data or information from standard practice in the field.

The proposed system incorporates a specialized hybrid reasoner [1] that integrates Rule-Based Reasoning (RBR), Case-Based Reasoning (CBR), and Process Mining. Process Mining focuses on the automated generation of process models from event-based data (e.g., recorded activities in information systems), which can then be analyzed to extract actionable insights and enhance the understanding of executed processes [21, 22].

The Process Mining layer of the hybrid-reasoner is not yet activated. It will be designed and evaluated in a future contribution, after a sufficient number of stored cases permits a valid Process Model to be built based on specific case attributes that represent certain actions happened after the decision has been taken. These actions actually constitute a process.

Based on this Process Model, Comp-DST can predict potential future scenarios that are justified by existing facts. For instance, the Process Mining layer can be designed to predict which decisions may be challenged in courts or to indicate the path of enabled transitions which predicts a possible series of implementation steps for the intervention-solution.

Disclosure of Interests. The authors have no competing interests to declare that are relevant to the content of this article.

References

1. Kaoura, G., Kovas, K., Boutsinas, B., Hatzilygeroudis, I.: A new hybrid reasoning model based on rules, cases and processes: application to care of individuals facing autism spectrum disorders. Knowl. Inf. Syst. **67**, 371–401 (2025)
2. La Noce, M.: Designing a management information system for competition law agencies. In: Di Bitetto, M., Chymis, A., D'Anselmi, P. (eds.) Public Management as Corporate Social Responsibility. CSR, Sustainability, Ethics & Governance, pp. 11–26. Springer, Cham (2015). https://doi.org/10.1007/978-3-319-07037-7_2
3. Computational Competition Law and Economics, An Inception Report (2021). https://www.epant.gr/files/2021/computational/computational_inception_report.pdf
4. EPANT homepage. www.epant.gr. Accessed 27 Apr 2025
5. ICN homepage, Agency Effectiveness. http://www.internationalcompetitionnetwork.org/working-groups/current/agency-effectiveness.aspx. Accessed 27 Apr 2025
6. EPANT homepage, Greek Law 3959/2011. https://www.epant.gr/nomothesia/nomoi-diatagmata/prostasia-antagonismoy.html. Accessed 27 Apr 2025
7. Articles 101 and 102 of the TFEU. https://eur-lex.europa.eu/legal-content/EN/TXT/PDF/?uri=CELEX:12012E/TXT. Accessed 27 Apr 2025
8. EPANT homepage, HCC Decision 844/2024. https://www.epant.gr/files/2024/apofaseis/844_2024.pdf. Accessed 27 Apr 2025
9. Zakim, D., Braun, N., Fritz, P., Alscher, M.D.: Underutilization of information and knowledge in everyday medical practice: evaluation of a computer-based solution. BMC Med. Inform. Decis. Mak. **8**, 50 (2008)
10. Prentzas, J., Hatzilygeroudis, I.: Categorizing approaches combining rule-based and case-based reasoning. Expert. Syst. **24**(2), 97–122 (2007)
11. Aamodt, A., Plaza, E.: Case-based reasoning: foundational issues, methodological variations, and system approaches. AI Commun. **7**, 39–59 (1994)
12. Eskin, E., Arnold, A., Prerau, M., Portnoy, L., Stolfo, S.: A geometric framework for unsupervised anomaly detection. In: Barbara, D., Jajodia, S. (eds.) Applications of Data Mining in Computer Security, pp. 78–100. Kluwer Academics (2002)
13. Wang, Y., Wang, X., Feng, Y., Liu, L.: Strategic response for ease of doing business using case-based reasoning. Expert Syst. Appl. **210**, 118514 (2022)
14. Boutsinas, B., Papastergiou, T.: On clustering tree structured data with categorical nature. Pattern Recogn. **41**(12), 3613–3623 (2008)
15. Jaccard, P.: Distribution de la flore alpine dans le bassin des dranses et dans quelques regions voisines. Bullet de la Société Vaudoise des Sci. Nat. **37**, 241–272 (1901)
16. Ligeza, A.: Logical Foundations for Rule-Based Systems. Studies in Computational Intelligence, vol. 11, pp. 189–211. Springer, Berlin (2006)
17. Buchanan, B.G., Smith, R.G.: Fundamentals of expert systems. Annu. Rev. Comput. Sci. **3**, 23–58 (1988)
18. Wagner, C.: Breaking the knowledge acquisition bottleneck through conversational knowledge management. Inf. Resour. Manag. J. **19**, 70–83 (2006)
19. Saba, W.: Did we just replace the 'knowledge bottleneck' with a 'data bottleneck'? Commun. ACM (2018). Accessed 27 Apr 2025
20. Freitas, A.A.: Understanding the crucial differences between classification and discovery of association rules: a position paper. SIGKDD Explor. Newsl. **2**(1), 65–69 (2000)
21. Van der Aalst, W.M.P.: Process Mining: Data Science in Action, 2nd edn., p. 5. Springer, Heidelberg (2016)
22. Van Der Aalst, W.M.P.: Object-centric process mining: unraveling the fabric of real processes. Mathematics **11**(12), 2691 (2023). Special Issue "Advances in Business Intelligence: Theoretical and Empirical Issues" (Ed. B. Boutsinas)

AI-Driven Approach to Image-Based Recognition

Virgilijus Sakalauskas[1(✉)], Dalia Kriksciuniene[2], and Paulius Baltrusaitis[1]

[1] Kauno kolegija, Pramones pr. 20, 50468 Kaunas, Lithuania
{virgilijus.sakalauskas,paulius.baltrusaitis}@go.kauko.lt
[2] Vilnius University, Universiteto St. 3, 01513 Vilnius, Lithuania
dalia.kriksciuniene@knf.vu.lt

Abstract. Image recognition systems based on digital photos are widely used in many areas—from security and healthcare to tracking wildlife or identifying lost pets. This paper presents a practical approach that uses artificial intelligence to handle recognition tasks. We combine deep learning methods for feature extraction with a similarity-based classification technique. As a real-world example, we built a system to recognize lost or homeless dogs using a structured image database. We used a pre-trained deep learning model (VGG16) to extract visual features from dog images and then applied the K-Nearest Neighbors (KNN) algorithm to match these features with those in the database. The study discusses key aspects like how the image dataset was prepared, how images were preprocessed, and how different similarity measures (Euclidean, Manhattan, and Cosine) were used to compare image features. Our test results showed that combining deep learning for feature extraction with a simple classifier like KNN worked well, even when the image quality varied. This type of system can be used in many other areas where visual recognition is needed and can be improved further with real-time processing or custom-trained deep learning models.

Keywords: artificial intelligence · data mining · image-based recognition · machine learning algorithms

1 Introduction

Image-based recognition has become an essential tool in many areas of artificial intelligence. It's used to recognise objects, animals, people, or scenes from images, and is widely applied in fields like security, healthcare, and environmental monitoring. Thanks to new developments in deep learning, especially with convolutional neural networks (CNNs), these systems can now achieve high accuracy in real-world tasks.

Models like VGG16, ResNet, and MobileNet have shown very strong results in image recognition tasks. These models are pre-trained on large datasets like ImageNet, which means they've already learned to detect useful patterns like edges, shapes, and textures [1, 2]. This makes them very good at extracting important features from new images. While these deep learning models are powerful, they can be hard to use in practical

K. Wącel (Ed.): BIS 2025 Workshops, LNBIP 568, pp. 64–74, 2026.
https://doi.org/10.1007/978-3-032-11651-2_6

systems because they often need a lot of computing power and well-labelled datasets [3].

In many cases, it helps to use a mix of deep learning and traditional machine learning. For example, we can use a CNN to extract features from images and then use a simpler method, like K-Nearest Neighbours (KNN), to match those features to known categories. This kind of hybrid approach can work well, especially when the dataset isn't very large and we need a method that's easier to manage and explain [4].

This paper presents a system that uses this hybrid method to identify lost or homeless dogs. The system was designed for use in an animal shelter, where new dogs are regularly photographed and added to a database. Using photos of these dogs, we extract features using a pre-trained CNN (VGG16), then match new images using KNN and similarity calculations to identify unknown dog photo.

The remainder of this paper is structured as follows: Sect. 2 introduces the similar research for recognizing lost or homeless dogs using a structured image database. Section 3 discusses dataset organization and preprocessing techniques for image recognition. Section 4 outlines the feature extraction and classification methodologies used in the system. Section 5 presents experimental results and evaluation metrics. Finally, Sect. 6 discusses challenges, potential improvements, and broader implications for AI-driven image recognition systems.

2 Literature Review

In this study, we focus on building an AI-based image recognition system to identify lost or homeless dogs by using a structured photo database. Many researchers have worked on related problems in recent years, and this section highlights some of their contributions.

In a 2023 study, Valarmathi et al. [5] compared several deep learning models for identifying dog breeds. They evaluated models like Xception, VGG19, NASNetMobile, EfficientNetV2M, ResNet152V2, and combinations like Inception + Xception. The goal was to find out which models perform best in breed classification tasks, and they discussed the pros and cons of each.

Another recent study by Tuteja et al. [6] focused on building a fine-grained image recognition system to classify different dog breeds. They used advanced convolutional neural networks (CNNs) and achieved high accuracy. This study showed how deep CNNs can improve classification in cases where different breeds look very similar.

Franzoni et al. [7] took a different approach. They used deep learning to analyze facial expressions in dogs to understand their emotions. Their system aimed to help humans better interpret dog behaviour, especially in recognising signs of aggression or friendliness. This research highlights how AI can support better human-animal interactions.

A study by Azizi et al. [8] worked on identifying lost pets. The researchers built a new dataset of cat and dog images and used transfer learning with different CNN architectures. Their goal was to speed up the process of locating lost pets, and their system showed good results in both species classification and identifying individual animals.

In earlier work, Mougeot et al. [9], developed a system for recognizing individual dogs using deep learning. Their system reached 92% accuracy in a dog face verification task, and 88% rank-5 accuracy in a one-shot recognition setup involving 48 different dogs. This study showed that it is possible to use AI for reliable individual dog identification.

These studies show that deep learning methods have made strong progress in recognizing and understanding dogs from images. From identifying breeds to emotions and individuals, CNN-based systems have become powerful tools. Transfer learning and pre-trained networks have also helped improve results without needing massive custom datasets.

Our research differs in several ways from the studies mentioned above:

- *Real-world focus*: Instead of focusing only on breed classification or academic datasets, our system is designed for use in a real animal shelter.
- *Simple and scalable*: We combine deep feature extraction using VGG16 with a basic KNN classifier. This makes it easier to update and use without retraining.
- *Unknown detection*: We include a threshold to detect unknown dogs, which many other systems do not handle.
- *User-friendly*: We built a graphical interface, making it easier for shelter staff to use without needing technical skills.
- *Individual identification*: Our goal is not to classify the breed, but to recognize individual dogs.

These distinctions highlight the system's equilibrium between accuracy, clarity & practical use in real-world scenarios. Although the focus is dog identification, the proposed method applies broadly to tasks like biometric authentication, industrial quality control & medical image analysis.

3 Dataset Organization and Pre-processing Steps

The performance of any image recognition system strongly depends on how the image data is organized and prepared. For our case study—identifying lost or homeless dogs—we used real-world data from the Penkta Koja (Fifth Leg) dog shelter in Lithuania. This shelter receives about 800 dogs each year, covering a wide variety of breeds, ages, and appearances. When a dog arrives at the shelter, it is photographed and registered. These photos make up the image database used in our system.

We arranged the shelter's image dataset into a hierarchical folder structure to smoothly handle and expand the data. Each folder in the main dataset directory holds pictures of a single dog. These folders are uniquely labelled "Dog1", "Dog2", etc. Every folder can have several photos of the same dog taken from different angles or in varying conditions. This setup makes feature extraction and label assignment straightforward during training and inference (See Fig. 1).

This structure helps in the following ways:

- It makes it easy to match images with dog identities.
- New dogs can be added by simply creating a new folder with their photos.

```
/dog_dataset/
   /Dog1/
      dog1_photo1.jpg
      dog1_photo2.jpg
      dog1_photo3.jpg
   /Dog2/
      dog2_photo1.jpg
      dog2_photo2.jpg
   /Dog3/
      dog3_photo1.jpg
      dog3_photo2.jpg
```

Fig. 1. Dog database structure

- It works well with many deep learning libraries that support folder-based labelling systems.

To keep image handling consistent before extracting features, all photos go through a standard preprocessing process to fit the deep learning model.

- **Resizing**: All images were resized to 224 × 224 pixels, which is the input size required by the VGG16 convolutional neural network. Using a fixed size ensures the model works properly and gets consistent input data.
- **Normalization**: The pixel values in the images, originally ranging from 0 to 255, were normalized. We used VGG16's standard preprocessing function, which scales and centres the pixel values. This improves the accuracy and stability of the model during feature extraction.

To carry out these steps, we used the Pillow (PIL) library in Python. This library works well with other tools like NumPy and integrates easily with deep learning frameworks.

By keeping the image data well-organized and applying the same preprocessing to every image, we ensured that the system could reliably extract features and perform accurate classification.

4 Feature Extraction and Classification Methodologies

The heart of our image recognition system is a hybrid method that combines deep learning for feature extraction and traditional machine learning for classification. This section explains how the system processes raw dog images, extracts useful data from them, and identifies the dog using those features.

To build the dog recognition system, we used the Python programming language. Python offers many powerful libraries for image processing, machine learning, and deep learning, which made it well suited for developing the system. The complete algorithm used in our system is shown in Fig. 2.

The first two steps—dataset arrangement and preprocessing—are already discussed. Now, we'll explain the four concluding steps of our system.

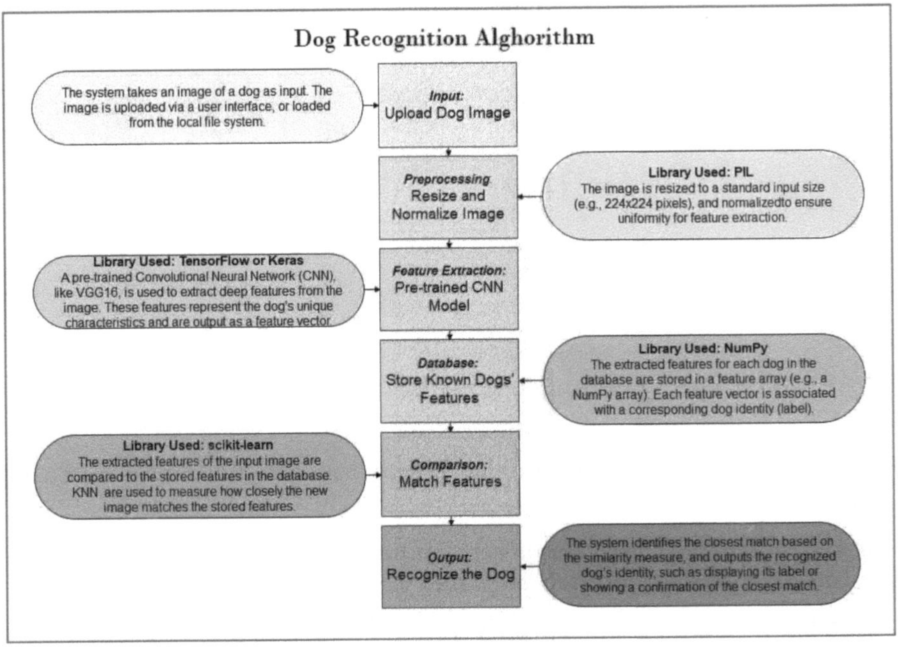

Fig. 2. The algorithmic steps of dog recognition system

Feature Extraction Using a Pretrained CNN

The goal of this step is to turn each image into a feature vector—a structured numerical format that represents the most important visual characteristics of the image. For this, we used the VGG16 model, a well-known deep learning architecture trained on the large ImageNet dataset (Simonyan & Zisserman, 2014).

VGG16 is a deep convolutional neural network made up of 16 layers. It is known for being simple yet effective in extracting image features for many tasks. In our system, we used VGG16 not for classification, but for feature extraction. This means we removed the final layers of the model that perform classification and kept only the layers that detect patterns.

Here is how the feature extraction works:

- Each image, resized to 224 × 224 pixels, is passed through the VGG16 model.
- The model outputs a high-dimensional feature vector, which contains data about textures, shapes, and spatial details of the image.
- We flatten this output into a one-dimensional array like this:

$$Feature\_vector = [0.12,\ 0.34,\ \ldots,\ 0.91].$$

This vector is a compact, informative summary of the dog image and forms the basis for classification in the next steps.

Feature Storage and Labeling

Each feature vector extracted from an image is stored together with a label, which identifies the dog (e.g., "Dog001", "Max", "Labrador_12"). We used NumPy arrays for storing the vectors efficiently. This allows for fast access and comparisons.

The storage structure is simple and flexible. It contains a set of feature vectors linked to a label that represents a known dog.

The database can easily be updated: when a new dog arrives, its image is processed the same way, and its features and label are added to the system.

Similarity-Based Classification with KNN

For classification, we used the K-Nearest Neighbors (KNN) algorithm. KNN is a simple, effective method that works especially well for small to medium-sized datasets, particularly when the feature vectors are well-organized by a strong model like VGG16.

Once the feature database is ready, we use the scikit-learn library in Python to compare a new dog's feature vector with all existing ones in the database.

Here's how the process works:

- The system calculates the **distance** (or similarity) between the new image's feature vector and every vector in the database.
- It selects the **K most similar vectors** (the nearest neighbors).
- It assigns the **label that occurs most often** among those K neighbors as the predicted identity of the dog.

KNN does not rely on just one match. Instead, it considers the closest K matches and uses a majority vote to decide. For example, if K = 3 and two of the nearest neighbors are labeled "Dog A", then the input image will be classified as "Dog A".

To compare vectors, we tested three commonly used similarity measures:

- *Euclidean Distance* is the straight-line distance between two vectors in the feature space.
- *Manhattan Distance* involves the sum of absolute differences between vector coordinates. Smaller figures indicate higher similarity.
- *Cosine Similarity* represents the cosine of the angle between two vectors, emphasizing their orientation in space, ranging between −1 and 1:

  - 1 denotes identical vectors.
  - 0 shows orthogonal vectors (no similarity).
  - −1 indicates opposite directions.

In practice, Euclidean distance has proven effective due to the normalized nature of feature vectors.

Output: Recognise the Dog

This final step produces the system's output. Based on the similarity scores, the KNN classifier selects the most likely match and returns that dog's identity from the database. The system also displays the matching dog's photo.

But sometimes, the dog might not exist in the database. In these cases, KNN will still return the closest match, even if it's not a real match. To handle this, we added a threshold. If the distance between the input vector and all database vectors is greater than 500, the system reports the result as "Unknown Dog".

This addition significantly improves the system's reliability and prevents incorrect identifications. It's especially useful in open-set recognition systems like ours, where new unknown examples can appear.

This blend—VGG16 extraction & KNN classification—provides an accurate, simple, & adaptable framework. This modular nature allows future enhancements, like switching classifiers or fine-tuning on specific data.

5 Experimental Results and Evaluation Metrics

To test how well our dog recognition system works in real-world conditions, we ran a set of experiments using actual data from the Penkta Koja dog shelter. We measured the system's ability to correctly identify known dogs and to recognize when a dog was not in the database.

We used the experimental two datasets of dog photos:

1. **Training set (known dogs):**

Photos of 126 dogs taken when they first arrived at the shelter. These images were used to build the feature database for recognition.

2. **Test set:**
   a) Photos of the same 126 dogs, but taken later, usually when the dogs were adopted. These images often had different angles, lighting, or grooming conditions.
   b) Photos of 126 different dogs who were not included in the training set.

This setup reflects a real-life use case. A known dog might return to the shelter or be seen on the street, and its image might look a little different. At the same time, new dogs not yet in the database need to be handled properly by the system.

Using temporally distinct photos of the same dogs, the system was tested for accuracy and its ability to handle intra-class variations. This approach offers a practical measure of how well the system can generalize across different instances of the same object, crucial for any image-based recognition system functioning in uncontrolled settings like animal shelters.

The image database was structured into subfolders for each dog, and feature vectors were extracted using the VGG16 convolutional neural network pretrained on ImageNet. These features were kept as NumPy arrays, with labels for each vector.

A K-Nearest Neighbors (KNN) classifier ($k = 3$) was trained on these features. The classification relied on described distance metrics in feature space. An extra distance threshold was applied (set empirically at 500) to differentiate between known and unknown dogs.

To gauge and compare system performance, we employed four evaluation metrics:

- Accuracy: The percentage of total images that were classified correctly.
- Precision: The proportion of correctly identified dogs out of all dogs predicted as "known".

- Recall: The proportion of correctly identified known dogs out of all actual known dogs.
- F1-Score: The harmonic mean of precision and recall, balancing their trade-off.

Using our image recognition program written in Python, we evaluated this system's performance based on a dataset of 126 known dogs (in the initial database) and 126 unknown dogs (not in the database). The original program can be downloaded using a link from the QR code:

Python needs to be installed along with required libraries to run this program, as is shown in Fig. 2.

When executed, it opens a Tkinter graphical interface that lets users:

- Select a folder with known dog images organized in subfolders.
- Pick an image of an unknown dog for recognition.

After choosing inputs and clicking "Recognize Dog," the program extracts features from the selected image and compares them to the known dataset using a KNN algorithm. If a match is within a specified distance threshold (e.g., 500), the application displays the recognized dog's name and image from the dataset with the calculated similarity distance (see Fig. 3).

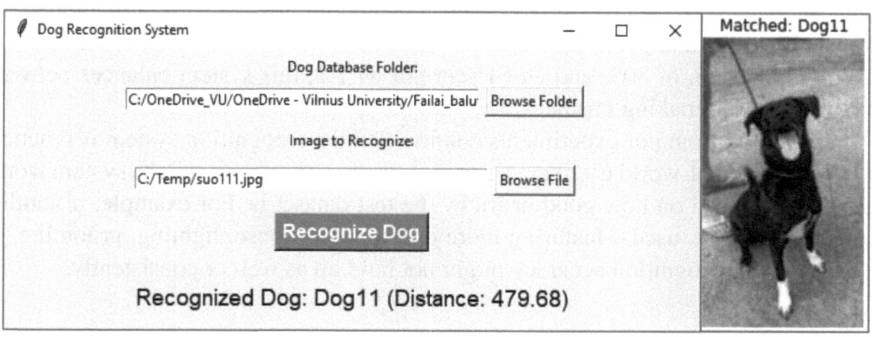

Fig. 3. Graphical interface for dog recognition system

If no close match is found within the set threshold, the program simply outputs "Unknown Dog". This tells us that the dog is probably not in the database.

We slightly modified the program to allow automatic testing of all 252 test images. This setup led to some interesting performance metrics (Table 1).

Table 1. Confusion Matrix

	Predicted Known	Predicted Unknown
Actual Known (126 dogs)	112	14
Actual Unknown (126 dogs)	28	98

When you look at the confusion matrix, the results of recognizing dogs appear pretty promising. For a more in-depth assessment of the system's performance, you can check out Table 2, which provides detailed evaluation metric values.

Table 2. Calculation performance metrics

Metric	Value
Accuracy	83.3%
Precision	80.0%
Recall (Sensitivity)	88.9%
Specificity	77.8%
F1 Score	84.2%

This experimental look into our proposed dog recognition system shows it's got a solid overall performance. This is backed up by the accuracy & other supporting metrics found in the confusion matrix.

The recognition system scored an overall accuracy of 83.3%. It managed to spot most dogs in the test group correctly. It accurately recognized 112 out of 126 known dogs (recall: 88.9%). This indicates it does well in matching dogs already in the database, even when lighting and posture change.

With a precision of 80% and an F1 score of 84.2%, this system balances between getting it right and making mistakes.

These results from our experiments confirm that the recognition system is practical and effective for real-world use. Yet, it's crucial to remember how well the system works might change based on how good or tricky the test dataset is. For example, if another set of dog images is used—featuring more differences in pose, lighting, grooming, or resolution—the recognition accuracy might not hold up as well or consistently.

6 Conclusion

This study introduced an artificial intelligence-based system for recognizing individual dogs using their images, with a focus on real-life application in a dog shelter environment. The system was designed to help identify lost or homeless dogs using photos taken at the shelter.

The approach combines deep learning for feature extraction and classical machine learning for classification. Specifically, we used a pre-trained VGG16 convolutional neural network to extract meaningful visual features from dog photos, and then used the K-Nearest Neighbors (KNN) algorithm to match those features with previously known dogs stored in the database.

Our experiments showed that this combination works well in practice. The system achieved an accuracy of 83.3% when tested on a dataset of 252 images, which included both known and unknown dogs. It was able to recognize individual dogs even when their photos were taken under different conditions, such as varying lighting, camera angles, and grooming states.

One of the strengths of the system is its simplicity and transparency:

- It does not require retraining when new dogs are added.
- It uses a basic, interpretable classifier (KNN).
- The graphical interface, built with Tkinter, makes it easy to use for non-technical users like shelter staff.

The system also includes a threshold mechanism to detect unknown dogs. This means that if a dog is not in the database, the system can report it as "unknown" rather than making a wrong identification. This is especially useful in real-world shelters where new animals arrive frequently.

However, we also identified some limitations. The system's accuracy depends on the quality and consistency of the images used during both training and testing. If the images vary too much in resolution, pose, or lighting, the recognition accuracy may decrease. To address this, future versions of the system could benefit from:

- Standardized photo-taking procedures (e.g., fixed background, lighting).
- Data augmentation techniques to make the system more robust.
- Fine-tuning of the VGG16 model on shelter-specific images.
- Replacing KNN with more advanced classifiers (like SVM or Siamese networks).

In conclusion, this work shows how existing AI tools and models can be effectively applied to real-world problems such as identifying lost animals. The system is flexible, easy to update, and accurate enough for practical use. Although our main focus was on dogs, the same method can be adapted for other image recognition tasks—such as medical imaging, biometric ID systems, industrial quality control, and more.

This research provides a strong foundation for future development and real-world deployment of visual recognition systems that are both simple to use and powerful in performance.

References

1. Simonyan, K., Zisserman, A.: Very deep convolutional networks for large-scale image recognition. arXiv preprint arXiv:1409.1556 (2014)
2. He, K., Zhang, X., Ren, S., Sun, J.: Deep residual learning for image recognition. In: Proceedings of the IEEE Conference on Computer Vision and Pattern Recognition (CVPR) (2016)

3. Deng, J., Dong, W., Socher, R., Li, L.-J., Li, K., Fei-Fei, L.: ImageNet: a large-scale hierarchical image database. In: IEEE Conference on Computer Vision and Pattern Recognition (CVPR) (2009)
4. Garcia-Gasulla, D., et al.: On the behavior of convolutional nets for feature extraction. J. Big Data **5**(1), 1–23 (2018)
5. Valarmathi, B., Gupta, N.S., Prakash, G., Reddy, R.H., Saravanan, S., Shanmugasundaram, P.: Hybrid deep learning algorithms for dog breed identification—a comparative analysis. IEEE Access **11**, 77228–77239 (2023). https://doi.org/10.1109/ACCESS.2023.3297440
6. Tuteja, A., Bathla, S., Jain, P., Garg, U., Dureja, A., Dureja, A.: Dog breed identification using deep learning. In: Swaroop, A., Polkowski, Z., Correia, S.D., Virdee, B. (eds.) ICDAM 2023. LNNS, vol. 785, pp. 515–530. Springer, Singapore (2024). https://doi.org/10.1007/978-981-99-6544-1_39
7. Franzoni, V., Biondi, G., Milani, A.: Advanced techniques for automated emotion recognition in dogs from video data through deep learning. Neural Comput. Appl. **36**, 17669–17688 (2024). https://doi.org/10.1007/s00521-024-10042-3
8. Azizi, E., Zaman, L.: Deep learning pet identification using face and body. Information **14**(5), 278 (2023). https://doi.org/10.3390/info14050278
9. Mougeot, G., Li, D., Jia, S.: A deep learning approach for dog face verification and recognition. In: Nayak, A., Sharma, A. (eds.) PRICAI 2019. LNCS, vol. 11672, pp. 418–430. Springer, Cham (2019). https://doi.org/10.1007/978-3-030-29894-4_34

SciBO-SEM 2025 – Workshop on Scientific Challenges and Business Opportunities in Sustainable Environmental Management

A Modular E-Learning Ecosystem for Green Entrepreneurship: Architecture, Implementation, and Personalization

Ştefănel Turcu[1], Alexandru Predescu[1](✉), Nirvana Popescu[1], Mariana Mocanu[1], and Ali Ganiyusufoğlu[2]

[1] Department of Computer Science, University POLITEHNICA, Bucharest, Romania
alexandru.predescu@upb.ro
[2] Selçuk University, Konya, Turkey

Abstract. Green entrepreneurship is emerging as a key driver for achieving sustainable development goals, while structured and personalized education pathways in this field remain limited. This paper presents the design and implementation of the Young Green Entrepreneurship Ecosystem e-Learning Platform, developed within the Erasmus+ Strategic Partnership project (2023-2-TR01-KA220-YOU-000185426). The platform offers a structured, modular, and scalable environment for delivering educational content to young entrepreneurs, mentors, angel investors, and green manufacturers. Built on a customized Moodle instance, the system integrates interactive content, gamification, and a novel recommendation plugin powered by machine learning. This work outlines the platform's conceptual framework, technical architecture, content management strategy, and personalization mechanisms. The proposed solution demonstrates how open-source LMS platforms can be extended with AI-driven features to support scalable, impactful, and engaging green entrepreneurship education.

Keywords: Green Entrepreneurship · E-Learning Platforms · Personalized Learning · Recommendation Systems

1 Introduction

Entrepreneurship education is recognized as a driver for innovation and sustainable economic growth [1]. As global challenges shift toward ecological concerns, green entrepreneurship plays a critical role in sustainable development and has gained increasing attention for achieving the Sustainable Development Goals (SDGs) by fostering environmentally conscious business practices and promoting systemic change [2, 3].

Despite the growing relevance of green entrepreneurship, young individuals often lack access to learning environments that reflect the cross-disciplinary, innovation-driven, and sustainability-focused nature of the field. Conventional entrepreneurship education tends to prioritize generic business skills without addressing the unique mindset, regulatory knowledge, and impact-driven strategies needed in green sectors [4].

K. Wącel (Ed.): BIS 2025 Workshops, LNBIP 568, pp. 77–87, 2026.
https://doi.org/10.1007/978-3-032-11651-2_7

Moreover, learning platforms often lack in support for adaptive, role-specific, and personalized pathways, especially those aligned with sustainability principles and career development.

Research in educational technology has shown that personalization and interactivity play a critical role in increasing learner motivation and engagement [5]. These insights are especially relevant for youth-centered programs, where learning effectiveness is closely tied to gamification, social learning, and dynamic content delivery [6].

To address these gaps, we introduce the YounGreenTeco e-Learning Platform: a digital environment specifically designed to empower aspiring green entrepreneurs, mentors, angel investors, and sustainable manufacturers. Developed as part of an Erasmus+ Strategic Partnership (2023-2-TR01-KA220-YOU-000185426), the platform integrates a modular content structure, personalized recommendation engine, and gamified progression system to deliver accessible, engaging, and pedagogically robust learning experiences.

Through this work, we aim to contribute to the advancement of e-learning systems that support inclusive and scalable green entrepreneurship education, aligned with contemporary digital learning and sustainability agendas [7]. This paper outlines the platform's conceptual framework, system architecture, content delivery mechanisms, and recommendation-based personalization features.

The main contributions of this work are: (1) implementation of a role-based LMS architecture for green entrepreneurship, (2) integration of semantic recommendation via contextual embeddings, and (3) design of a scalable plugin-driven Moodle enhancement strategy.

The remainder of this paper is structured as follows: Sect. 2 reviews related work on learning management systems, gamification in e-learning, and personalized recommendation engines; Sect. 3 presents the methodological framework adopted for the platform's development and evaluation; Sect. 4 describes the system architecture and implementation in detail, including the content management strategy and personalization engine; Sect. 5 summarizes the findings and challenges encountered during the project rollout; and finally, Sect. 6 concludes with future directions for enhancing green entrepreneurship education through AI-driven personalization, adaptive sequencing, and deeper integration with emerging digital ecosystems.

2 Related Work

Prior research highlights the benefits of Learning Management Systems (LMS) in structuring knowledge and enhancing learner engagement [5]. Learning Management Systems (LMS) are effective tools for delivering structured educational content and enabling learner engagement, particularly in digital and distance education settings [5]. Among LMS platforms, Moodle stands out due to its open-source nature, community support, and modular architecture, which supports extensive customization, and has been adopted in various educational contexts [8].

While studies have examined the role of e-learning in entrepreneurship education [9], few have explored domain-specific implementations focused on sustainability and adaptive personalization. For example, GreenLearning.ca provides structured online resources in environmental education, but lacks adaptive personalization. In contrast, our platform integrates machine learning to tailor content to user profiles, providing both sustainability-oriented and learner-centric delivery.

Personalization in e-learning is a growing field, with recommender systems being commonly employed to address the issue of information overload and enhance learner motivation and performance. Efforts to enhance its personalization capabilities have included recommender systems [10] and gamification strategies [6].

Content-based filtering approaches, such as those using TF-IDF and cosine similarity, have shown promise in modeling user preferences and course characteristics [10, 11]. Other studies have explored the use of ontology-based and hybrid recommenders to tailor learning content [10]. Our platform builds upon these foundations by combining structured user profiles with a machine learning-enhanced recommendation engine.

Gamification is another widely explored avenue to boost engagement and motivation in educational environments. Empirical studies have demonstrated that gamified elements, such as points, badges, and leaderboards, can improve completion rates and learner satisfaction [6]. By integrating gamification within the Moodle ecosystem, our approach aligns with recent findings that suggest these mechanisms are particularly effective when linked with meaningful learning activities.

In the domain of entrepreneurship education, prior research indicates a significant positive correlation between structured educational interventions and entrepreneurial intention [9]. However, most implementations have focused on traditional entrepreneurship or generalized business skills, with limited attention to sustainability-focused curricula or platform-driven delivery models. The YounGreenTeco platform addresses this gap by contextualizing green entrepreneurship within a digital learning framework.

Thus, our work contributes to the intersection of LMS design, recommender systems, and entrepreneurship education by offering a domain-specific, scalable, and intelligent platform aligned with current best practices in educational technology.

3 Methodology

The proposed methodological approach is aimed at solving identified organizational or educational problems by leveraging LMS design, and addresses the following research items:

- **Problem identification:**
- The lack of accessible, structured, and context-specific digital resources for green entrepreneurship training was identified through needs assessments within the Erasmus+ partnership.
- **Proposed solution definition:** Based on stakeholder input (students, educators, institutions), the platform was designed to fulfill several key goals: provide modular and scalable learning paths; support diverse learner profiles and roles (entrepreneurs, mentors, angel investors, manufacturers, course admin); enable personalized course recommendations based on interests and prior activity; and encourage learner retention and engagement through gamification.

- **Technical design:** The platform was implemented using Moodle 4.x as a foundation, with custom plugins developed in PHP for enforcing profile completeness and tracking user preferences. The recommendation system was implemented using Python scripts leveraging TF-IDF and cosine similarity. These components were integrated through Moodle's plugin API and deployed on cloud infrastructure.
- **Deployment:** The platform was deployed and piloted across several educational institutions involved in the Erasmus+ project. Stakeholders were invited to test various roles and provide feedback. Learning content was created using multimedia templates, while quizzes were deployed using Moodle's quiz engine.
- **Evaluation:** Evaluation was based on both qualitative feedback (e.g., surveys, interviews) and quantitative analytics (e.g., course completions, recommendation usage, quiz performance). While the platform supports collection of qualitative feedback via surveys and interviews, the current evaluation scope primarily reflects quantitative analytics.
- **Communication:** The results of this project, including its architectural design, plugin codebase, and pedagogical strategies, are documented and shared through open repositories (e.g., GitHub), transnational project meetings, conference presentations, and project dissemination activities.

The methodology follows an iterative approach, allowing the system to evolve based on stakeholder participation and dynamic scenarios. It also ensures that technical decisions are aligned with learning and user interactions, providing a user-centered design process supported by the personalization capabilities of the LMS.

4 Solution Architecture and Implementation

The YounGreenTeco platform is structured as a modular, role-driven ecosystem built upon Moodle and hosted on a cloud infrastructure. The architecture integrates learning content management, personalized recommendation logic, and gamified progress tracking within a secure and extensible environment. The structure is aligned with the layered design depicted in Fig. 1.

4.1 System Architecture

The Moodle UI encompasses the main user-facing components: user profile, dashboard, and courses. These modules allow users to define their learning journey, manage preferences, and access learning materials.

The web interface is delivered through the Moodle UI, themed with custom layouts for enhanced usability, and provides the main dashboard personalized for each user category, course listing, lesson navigation, and progress overview. The user roles and permissions are implemented using Moodle's built-in roles system. Each user is assigned one or more primary roles (Student, Teacher, Admin), with associated capabilities.

Custom profile fields (role, institution, interests) were added to extend the default user schema with the roles required in the project (Entrepreneur, Mentor, Angel Investor, Manufacturer) and their affiliations (institutions), to enable recommendation logic and advanced filtering. In terms of content management, the courses are organized into categories (Entrepreneurship, Mentorship, Angel Investment, Manufacturing), with each course containing multiple lessons, multimedia components, quizzes, and completion rules.

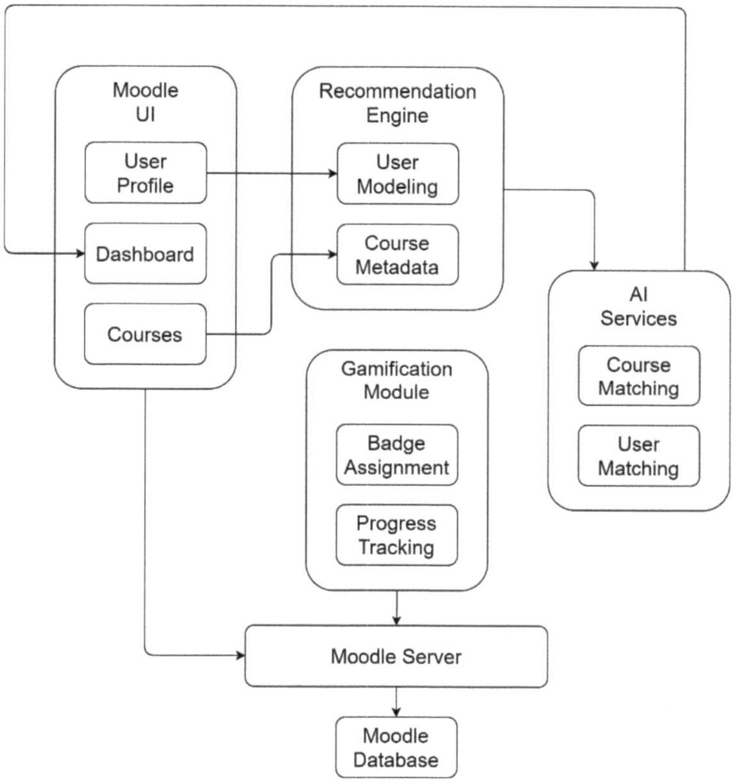

Fig. 1. System Architecture

To allow for more advanced functionality and further customization, Moodle's core codebase is augmented by custom plugins and external scripts, which are organized in a GitHub repository for collaborative development and version control. A custom plugin enforces profile completeness and feeds user data into the recommender system, which outputs personalized course suggestions displayed on the user dashboard. The recommendation engine is implemented as a hybrid plugin calling a Python script from within Moodle (via PHP). User profiles and course metadata (title, description, topics) are processed through a TF-IDF model to compute content similarity.

The user profile data and course descriptions are channeled into the Recommendation Engine, which gathers user interests and course metadata to form input vectors. The vectors are sent to the AI Services component implemented via a PHP-Python bridge. The results are filtered and ranked before being displayed on the user's Dashboard via a custom block. The following steps outline the processing pipeline in the recommendation plugin:

- The PHP plugin collects user profile data and completed courses.
- A background process calls the Python-based recommendation script.
- The script parses course description and user vectors, computes similarity scores, and returns a ranked list of course IDs: vectorizes input with scikit-learn TF-IDF, computes pairwise semantic similarity, filters enrolled courses, outputs ranked list of recommendations.
- The results are rendered dynamically in the Moodle UI via a custom block.

The personalization engine computes user-course similarity by generating contextual embeddings of user interests and course descriptions, then computing cosine similarity. This method follows established practices in content-based filtering [11], adapted for educational domains.

New features, such as the upcoming social networking module, are supported by Moodle's plugin-based design and the Python bridge. The proposed architecture anticipates future integrations with chat tools, peer-matching systems, and advanced analytics dashboards that can be supported by the powerful Python ecosystem in terms of data processing frameworks.

Simultaneously, the Gamification Module, which includes Badge Assignment and Progress Tracking, is designed within the Moodle environment to enhance learner engagement. The gamification layer integrates Moodle's native badge system. Students earn badges by completing lessons, passing quizzes, or finishing entire courses. Admins configure badge conditions and visuals using the badge management interface.

All components interface with the Moodle server directly, which enforces access control and orchestrates system operations. The server communicates directly with the Moodle database, ensuring consistent storage of all user activity, course configurations, and recommendation data. The entire workflow reflects a tightly integrated architecture optimized for personalized, data-driven, and gamified e-learning experiences.

4.2 AI Service

In this section, two recommendation techniques were compared: a traditional content-based filtering method using cosine similarity, and a semantic similarity approach leveraging pre-trained language models. From the implementation perspective, the AI service is built using Python and exposes an endpoint for generating course recommendations via the Flask library. The application consists of two endpoints: the main one used for recommendations, and another for service health checks.

To recommend the most relevant articles for the user, we initially applied a cosine similarity approach, i.e., a method that transforms both the user profile information and course descriptions into numerical vectors. The technique calculates the cosine of the angle between these vectors; the closer the angle is to zero, the more similar the two are. Although this technique is simple and often effective, it is strongly tied on overlapping terms. As a result, its effectiveness can be limited when the vocabulary varies significantly between the inputs, i.e., in our case, the course content and the user profile [11].

To validate the effectiveness of the solution, we created a set of input files, using ChatGPT to generate a variety of user profiles. We then measured the similarity between the top recommended courses and the user's existing profile and completed courses. Each term is weighted using Term Frequency-Inverse Document Frequency (TF-IDF) to reduce the impact of common terms:

$$TF\text{-}IDF(t,d) = tf(t,d) \cdot log\left(\frac{N}{df(t)}\right) \tag{1}$$

The similarity score between a user profile vector u and a course vector c is computed using cosine similarity:

$$S_C(u,c) = \frac{u \cdot c}{\|u\|\|c\|} \tag{2}$$

This metric produces values in the range $[-1, 1]$, where a value closer to 1 indicates a high degree of similarity.

To assess the effectiveness of this baseline approach, we generated 30 user profiles. For each profile, we measured the similarity score between the profile vector and the recommended course vectors. The overall average similarity score across all test cases was calculated as:

$$\frac{1}{n}\sum\nolimits_{i=1}^{n} S_C(u_i, c_i) \tag{3}$$

On average, the cosine similarity approach yielded a similarity score of 0.1159 across all 30 prepared inputs. The approach assumes that a score below 0.29 indicates very low similarity, likely irrelevant or unrelated, while a score above 0.7 is generally considered acceptable for identifying strong similarity. In our case, the best score obtained using this approach was 0.2683.

The second approach to implementing the course recommendation system involved adding an extra step before the cosine similarity calculation by introducing a semantic matching model. This method uses language models to capture the meaning behind words and phrases, enabling more accurate matching between the user profile and course content. It goes a step beyond the simpler keyword-overlap approach. While the first solution vectorized the input using traditional techniques, this approach builds the vectors using a deep language model, making the comparisons meaning-aware rather than purely word-based [12].

The user and course representations are thus defined as:

$u = f(user\ profile\ text)$
$v = f(course\ description\ text)$

where $f(\cdot)$ is the embedding function of the language model.

These embeddings are compared using cosine similarity, just like in the baseline method, but now the similarity is based on contextual meaning rather than exact word overlap. Using the same testing approach with the previously created inputs, the average similarity score for the entire dataset increased to 0.5006, representing a significant improvement given the limited content available on the platform.

Overall, adopting a semantic similarity model in the course recommendation solution brought a substantial improvement over the initial keyword-based method by capturing contextual meaning rather than relying solely on term overlap. The semantic model improved average similarity scores from 0.1159 to 0.5006, offering more contextually aligned recommendations. The system now delivers more relevant and accurate recommendations, enhancing the learning experience by better aligning with user preferences.

4.3 Content Management

The content management strategy in the YounGreenTeco platform is defined as a modular, template-based structure that supports clarity, interactivity, and consistency across courses. Each course is aligned with defined learning paths and designed to accommodate young entrepreneurs and educators. The curricula (Entrepreneurship, Mentoring, Angel Investment, Manufacturing) is defined using course categories, and the modules are defined as courses, such as depicted in Fig. 2. The home page was then configured to show the categories using a combo list layout.

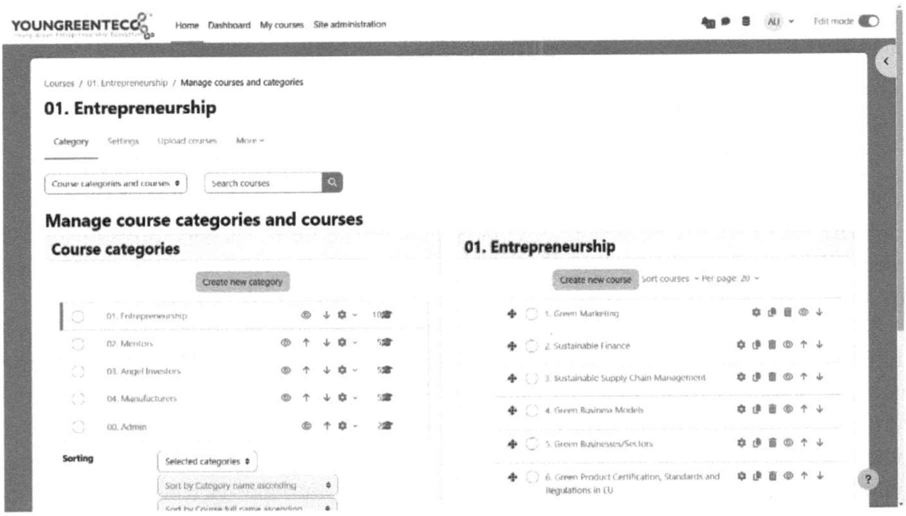

Fig. 2. Managing courses and modules

Following the introduction, each course presents an overview and learning objectives, sequential lessons with text, multimedia, and external resources to enrich the content and stimulate learner engagement. The course metadata (topics) are aligned with learner profiles to improve recommendation accuracy, while the learning content is structured using Moodle Lessons or can be provided as documents.

Lessons can be configured using the Moodle editor, as shown in Fig. 3 while the content can be provided directly from template documents allowing for collaborative editing before uploading it into the platform.

The quizzes are defined and uploaded into Moodle question bank using a Python script. The quiz engine supports retry logic, feedback, and grading. The completion criteria and badges are defined for each course to enable progress tracking and gamified scenarios.

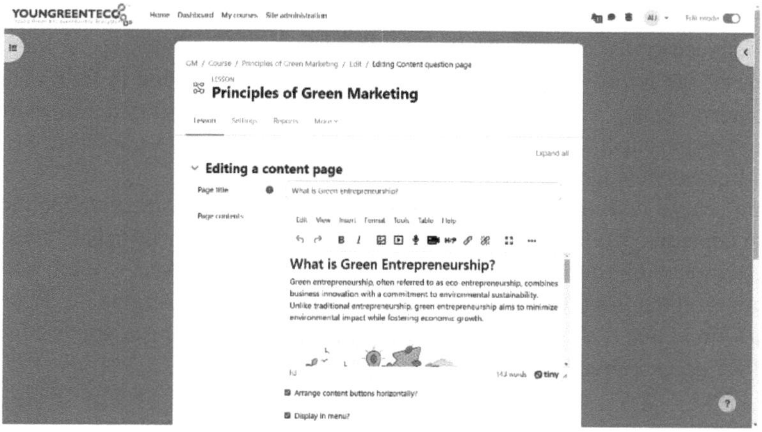

Fig. 3. Lesson content editor

The platform is deployed on a Linux-based cloud instance. Regular backup scripts (cron jobs) handle MySQL database backup and tar archiving for the codebase and data file system, respectively.

5 Results and Discussion

This project contributes to the body of work on domain-specific e-learning systems by:

- Proposing a modular approach to green entrepreneurship education
- Demonstrating the integration of Moodle with AI-based personalization
- Supporting user engagement through gamified learning and intelligent recommendations

Some of the challenges encountered were regarding content creation which involved a large number of courses drafted by multiple participants. The course materials were drafted by the participants using a document template. While the content should be properly formatted (headings and normal text) before uploading into the Moodle Lesson editor, ensuring consistency proved to be a challenge. As the Moodle Editor will pick up the formatting from the document headings, the original structure of the course is later difficult to determine unless properly formatted in the original document. Other challenges involve plugin maintenance, multilingual content delivery, and balancing user freedom with structured learning paths.

The results obtained through the evaluation of the recommendation engine demonstrate the advantages of incorporating semantic matching techniques into the platform's personalization pipeline. The baseline approach using TF-IDF and cosine similarity produced limited relevance in recommendations, while the adoption of a semantic similarity model substantially improved the system's ability to connect user profiles with meaningful course content. This improvement can be attributed to the semantic model's capacity to capture contextual meaning rather than relying solely on surface-level term overlap. The semantic model substantially improved the relevance of course suggestions, which is essential in interdisciplinary domains where learners use diverse vocabularies and express nuanced goals.

However, the improvements observed must also be considered in light of the platform's current scale, as the semantic model's reliance on external pre-trained language models introduces considerations around computational cost, inference time, and potential biases embedded in the training data.

Overall, these findings support the perspectives of semantic recommendation techniques for educational personalization. They also emphasize the need to balance technical implementation with usability. The integration of AI-driven personalization, when combined with modular content structure and gamified learning, positions the YounGreenTeco platform in line with sustainability and innovation goals of an adaptive educational platform for green entrepreneurship.

6 Conclusion and Future Work

This paper presented the design, implementation, and evaluation of the YounGreenTeco platform, as a modular e-learning system tailored for green entrepreneurship education. Built on top of Moodle and enhanced with AI capabilities, the platform integrates personalized course recommendations, gamified progression, and structured content delivery to support the development of entrepreneurial skills with a focus on sustainability.

The recommendation engine provides support for aligning e-learning content with user interests and backgrounds. By comparing a traditional approach with a semantic embedding model, the study demonstrated the significant benefits of using contextual language representations in recommender systems in this domain.

Although this study is limited by the small sample size during pilot evaluation, future iterations aim to conduct broader user studies and gather real-time usage metrics within the Erasmus+ partner institutions involved in this project.

The modularity and open-source integration of the proposed architecture facilitate future scalability and cross-institutional use, which are key for projects with international participation. Future development will focus on:

- adaptive lesson sequencing based on learner progress and competencies;
- peer-to-peer learning features such as networking, and mentoring;
- competency modeling with sustainability frameworks and professional skillsets.

Ultimately, the YounGreenTeco platform illustrates how open-source educational infrastructure can be enhanced with AI-driven personalization to support sustainable development goals, entrepreneurial education, and inclusive digital learning.

Acknowledgments. This research was carried out as part of the YounGreenTeco project, funded under the Erasmus+ Strategic Partnership programme (Project Code: 2023-2-TR01-KA220-YOU-000185426). The authors would like to thank all project partners, contributors, and participating institutions for their collaboration and support in the development, deployment, and evaluation of the e-learning platform.

Disclosure of Interests. The authors declare that they have no competing interests relevant to the content of this article.

References

1. Gibb, A.: In pursuit of a new 'enterprise' and 'entrepreneurship' paradigm for learning: creative destruction, new values, new ways of doing things and new combinations of knowledge. Int. J. Manag. Rev. **4**, 233–269 (2002). https://doi.org/10.1111/1468-2370.00086
2. Cohen, B., Winn, M.I.: Market imperfections, opportunity and sustainable entrepreneurship. J. Bus. Ventur. **22**, 29–49 (2007)
3. Aras, G., Crowther, D.: Making Ecopreneurs: Developing Sustainable Entrepreneurship. Gower Publishing, Ltd. (2012)
4. Lans, T., Blok, V., Wesselink, R.: Learning apart and together: towards an integrated competence framework for sustainable entrepreneurship in higher education. J. Clean. Prod. **62**, 37–47 (2014)
5. Graf, S., Kinshuk, Liu, T.-C.: Supporting teachers in identifying students' learning styles in learning management systems: an automatic student modelling approach. J. Educ. Technol. Soc. **12**, 3–14 (2009)
6. Domınguez, A., Saenz-de Navarrete, J., De-Marcos, L., Fernández-Sanz, L., Pagés, C., Martınez-Herráiz, J.-J.: Gamifying learning experiences: practical implications and outcomes. Comput. Educ. **63**, 380–392 (2013)
7. Wals, A.E., Kieft, G.: Education for sustainable development: research overview (2010)
8. Dougiamas, M., Taylor, P.: Moodle: using learning communities to create an open source course management system. In: EdMedia+ Innovate Learning, pp. 171–178. Association for the Advancement of Computing in Education (AACE) (2003)
9. Nabi, G., Liñán, F., Fayolle, A., Krueger, N., Walmsley, A.: The impact of entrepreneurship education in higher education: a systematic review and research agenda. Acad. Manag. Learn. Educ. **16**, 277–299 (2017)
10. Tarus, J.K., Niu, Z., Mustafa, G.: Knowledge-based recommendation: a review of ontology-based recommender systems for e-learning. Artif. Intell. Rev. **50**, 21–48 (2018)
11. Ricci, F., Rokach, L., Shapira, B.: Introduction to recommender systems handbook. In: Ricci, F., Rokach, L., Shapira, B., Kantor, P. (eds.) Recommender Systems Handbook, pp. 1–35. Springer, Boston (2011). https://doi.org/10.1007/978-0-387-85820-3_1
12. Huang, R.: Improved content recommendation algorithm integrating semantic information. J. Big Data. **10**, 84 (2023)

Activity-Based Cost and Scope 3-GHG Accounting

Walter S. A. Schwaiger[1(✉)] and Jeremias Meyer[2]

[1] Institute of Management Science, TU-Wien, Theresianumgasse 27, 1040 Vienna, Austria
walter.schwaiger@tuwien.ac.at

[2] Research Institute for Cooperation and Cooperatives, WU-Wien, Welthandelsplatz 1, 1020 Vienna, Austria
jeremias.meyer@wu.ac.at

Abstract. This paper proposes an integrated framework for Scope 3-greenhouse gas (GHG) emission accounting by aligning the Greenhouse Gas Protocol (GHGP) with Activity-Based Costing (ABC) methods. Scope 3-GHG emissions, which occur outside organizational boundaries, are often difficult to allocate accurately, leading to inconsistencies between corporate and product-level carbon reporting - a problem known as the 'divergence problem.' By conceptualizing all 15 Scope 3 categories within a Unified Modeling Language (UML) activity diagram, this paper offers a methodology to connect emissions with resource consumption (e.g., materials, energy, labor, equipment). The framework distinguishes between attributable and non-attributable emissions to provide compliance with the GHGP and introduces a 2-tiered accounting system: one for product-level reporting and the other for corporate reporting and internal decision-making. This system improves transparency, supports decision-making, and lays the groundwork for integration into enterprise resource planning (ERP) systems. The findings highlight the potential of activity-based approaches for aligning emissions and cost data, thereby enhancing both environmental performance and regulatory compliance.

Keywords: Activity-based costing · Scope 3 emissions · divergence problem

1 Introduction

Addressing climate change is one of the most critical challenges of our time, which drives the need to reduce greenhouse gas (GHG) emissions across industries, products, and supply chains to achieve a sustainable future [1]. In response, global frameworks such as the Greenhouse Gas Protocol (GHGP) have become increasingly central to standardizing emissions reporting [2]. The GHGP introduces a classification system into Scope 1, Scope 2, and Scope 3 emissions, and forms the basis for disclosure standards, including the European Sustainability Reporting Standard (ESRS) [3] and the International Sustainability Standards Board (ISSB) S2 by the IFRS Foundation [4].

While Scope 1, direct greenhouse gas emissions, derive from the combustion of oil, gas, and other fossil fuels within the organizational boundaries, Scope 2 emissions are

K. Wącel (Ed.): BIS 2025 Workshops, LNBIP 568, pp. 88–100, 2026.
https://doi.org/10.1007/978-3-032-11651-2_8

emitted due to the amount of electric energy used by the regarded company [5]. The 'Corporate Value Chain (Scope 3) Accounting and Reporting Standard [6]' (GHGP-Scope3-Standard), also published by the GHGP Initiative, outlines the reporting of Scope 3, the indirect emissions, are emitted outside of the organizational boundaries of the reporting organization. They can be divided into 15 categories and appear either upstream (Purchased goods and services; Employee commuting ...) or downstream within the value chain of the company [6]. Scope 3 reporting is also closely related to the calculation of product carbon footprints, as outlined in the GHGP's 'Product Life Cycle Accounting and Reporting Standard [7]' (GHGP-Product-Standard).

However, the reliability and comparability of Scope 3 reporting remains limited. The reporting of Scope 3 emissions is criticized for the low comparability of the metrics [8] and the frequent usage of average data [9, 10] in the underlying accounting systems.

The usage of industry-wide average data instead of an accurate allocation of Scope 3 emissions can weaken incentives for organizations to engage environmentally superior suppliers or make effective mitigation decisions [9]. Moreover, the lack of harmonization between product-level and corporate-level carbon accounting has led to what is referred to as the 'divergence problem' [11] of product and corporate carbon footprint (CF). So far, the integration of product and corporate CF has only been addressed within the context of the ISO-Standardization [11] or has only been addressed from an overly simplistic perspective, stating that the 'sum of all products and service carbon footprints is equal to the total carbon footprint of the associated organization [12].' In their literature review and research agenda, [2] emphasize the need to improve the transparency and accounting of Scope 3 emissions to increase the company's carbon performance by target setting, monitoring, and directing emission reduction improvements. To facilitate an integrated view of Scope 3 reporting and accounting, recent literature emphasizes the potential of activity-based emission accounting to integrate cost- and emission accounting and align emission data with decision-making processes [10, 13–15]. Existing approaches towards the integration of emission reporting into activity-based accounting systems only take Scope 3 Category 1 (Purchased goods and services) and Category 2 (Capital goods) into account [10, 14, 15].

This paper contributes to the field of carbon emission accounting integration by addressing four distinct aspects: First (1) it proposes a conceptual model in UML-activity-diagram that enables the integrability of all 15 Scope 3 emission categories into an activity-based emission and cost accounting system, aligned with GHGP principles. The analysis is based on the manufactured products, which serve as a reference point for assessing the company's activities. By revealing the underlying activities (2) behind the 15 Scope 3 categories, it opens the debate on activity-based Scope 3 emission measurement [cf. 14] outside of the organization's operational boundaries. Using business information systems that foster interorganizational information exchange, consumption-based CF could be calculated in the future. Third (3), this approach clarifies the 'divergence problem' [11] of product and corporate-level carbon in the context of the GHGP. Fourth (4), the conceptualization reveals legislative problems within the current reporting of Scope 3 accounting. The ongoing research focuses on the integration of the conceptual model into an integrated cost- and emission accounting business information system.

The remainder of the paper is structured as follows: Sect. 2 reviews current research on the integration of emissions reporting into activity-based reporting systems. In Sect. 3, the integration of Scope 3-GHG emissions into activity-based costing systems is conceptualized using a UML-activity-diagram. This conceptual work lays the foundation for further integration of all 15 Scope 3 emission categories. Section 4 discusses the practical and theoretical limitations of a fully integrated view of Scope 3 emissions. The paper concludes with a summary and implications for future research.

2 GHG Accounting: Theoretical Background

To develop an integrated approach for Scope 3-GHG emission accounting, this section outlines the relevant theoretical foundations. It first introduces the structure and challenges of Scope 3 reporting under the GHGP, then reviews activity-based approaches to cost and emission accounting.

2.1 Scope 3-GHG Emission and Product-Level Accounting

Within the GHGP-Scope3-Standard, 15 different categories of Scope 3-GHG emissions are specified [6]. The categories can be distinguished between emissions appearing upstream and downstream in the value chain. Table 1 gives an overview of the 15 different Scope 3 categories. It is important to highlight that Scope 3 emissions are not emitted within the reporting company's facilities but outside of their direct organizational boundary. For the boundary setting, the GHGP3-Standard proposes three different approaches: equity share, in which a company accounts for GHG emissions from operations according to its share of equity in the operation, financial control, in which the company accounts for the GHG emissions over which it has financial control, and operational control, in which a company accounts for the emissions over which it has operational control [6, p. 29]. The correct boundary setting is therefore crucial for determining which emissions appear as Scope 1, Scope 2, and which as Scope 3-GHG emissions in reporting.

While the assessment of corporate CF is historically rooted in the context of emission trading [16] the product CF is rooted in the context of Life-Cycle Assessment (LCA) [17, 18]. Due to the increasing importance of company emission reporting, accounting frameworks as the GHGP are of increasing importance [2], which pushes the relevance of LCA reporting, which is based on the ISO-LCA standard [19] into the background. In contrast to the corporate-related 15 Scope 3 categories, the GHGP-Product-Standard provides for 5 distinct life cycle stages, including the (I) material acquisition and pre-processing, the (II) production, the (III) distribution and storage, (IV) the use-phase and the (V) end-of-life treatment of the product. Whether carbon emissions are included in the CF of the product, the GHGP-Product-Standard differentiates between *attributable* and *non-attributable* processes. While *attributable* processes are defined as 'service, material, and energy flows that become the product, make the product, and carry the product through its life cycle' [7, p. 135], *non-attributable* processes are 'processes and services, materials and energy flows [that] are not directly connected to the studied product because they do not become the product, make the product, or directly carry the product through its life cycle' [7, p. 135]. According to [7, p. 36] *non-attributable* emissions include 'capital goods (e.g., machinery, trucks, infrastructure), overhead operations (e.g., facility lighting, air conditioning), corporate activities and services (e.g., research and development, administrative functions, company sales and marketing), transport of the product user to the retail location, [and] transport of employees to and from work.' Allocation of *non-attributable* emissions to the products is not planned. The GHGP-Product-Standard only describes allocations if several products result from one process.

Table 1. Overview of 15 Scope 3-GHG emission categories derived from [6, p. 5]

Upstream	Cat. 1	Purchased Goods and Services
	Cat. 2	Capital Goods
	Cat. 3	Fuel- and energy-related activities (not included in Scope 1 or Scope 2)
	Cat. 4	Upstream transportation and distribution
	Cat. 5	Waste generated in operations
	Cat. 6	Business Travel
	Cat. 7	Employee commuting
	Cat. 8	Upstream leased assets
Downstream	Cat. 9	Downstream transportation and distribution
	Cat. 10	Processing of sold products
	Cat. 11	Use of sold products
	Cat. 12	End-of-life treatment of sold products
	Cat. 13	Downstream leased assets
	Cat. 14	Franchises
	Cat. 15	Investments

2.2 Activity-Based GHG Emission Accounting

Within all three GHGP standards, an 'activity-based approach' is identified as the preferred method for assessing GHG emissions at the corporate, product, and value chain level [5–7]. This methodological preference is grounded in the general cause-and-effect relationship that emerges when emissions are attributed to discrete activities. In comparison to the usage of industry-wide average data [9], the usage of activity data grounds the core of managing GHG emissions by changing the characteristics of the emission-driving activities. The general logic is grounded in Leontief's input-output production theory [20] that links cost accounting and production systematization.

The usage of activity data in the field of sustainability accounting can further build on the academic contributions of the Activity-based costing (ABC) literature [21, 22]. Initially, ABC is a cost accounting system with a focal point on overhead costs, which are allocated to the produced goods using a consumption-oriented approach rather than a volume-based approach. Within ABC, resources are assigned to activities, and the activities are then assigned to the production of individual products. In comparison to volume-based cost allocation, the ABC system enables a 2-fold perspective on the cost of the processes and the cost of the produced products. The initial logic of ABC was supplemented by the Time-Driven-ABC (TD-ABC) logic, which introduces production functions to simplify the cost accounting system [22].

The positive synergy of activity-based cost accounting and environmental accounting was first highlighted by Stuart et al. [23] and further developed by [24]. While the developments in [23] follow a normative nature of research, more practical and holistic approaches integrating eco-efficiency, total quality, and overall sustainability emerged in the research field [25]. Stuart [23] contrasts the allocation of waste using a traditional volume-based method with an activity-based allocation method. Emblemsvåg and Bras [24] point out that the concept of ABC can be used to cover other resource consumption next to financial aspects, by using the same input-output logic as in the financial accounting system. This is illustrated by examining energy consumption and waste management within the ABC framework, underscoring the benefits of an integrated system that addresses both financial and non-financial aspects rather than relying on separate approaches for each. Instead of just reporting non-financial issues, the integrated ABC helps to identify ways to improve sustainability and environmental performance [24].

Duran and Afonso [26] take up the concept of Activity-based Life Cycle Costing and provide a model for managing spare part logistics, while Yang [27] calculated the CF of green energy supply using ABC, offering a tool to compare the CF per kWh produced. Similarly, Kayrbekova [28] provides an activity-based life cycle costing methodology that might be used to plan production facilities, deriving the costs arising from environmental aspects within the life cycle. An integrated approach of activity-based LCA is provided by [29] streamlining the allocation of environmental impacts to products. However, this methodology needs to be reviewed in the context of the GHGP.

Due to its systematic nature, ABC is noted for its potential integration into green information systems [30]. GHG emissions are explicitly considered within a Green Activity-based Management methodology following the conceptualization of the GHGP with the subdivision into Scope 1, Scope 2, and Scope 3 emissions [15]. Although Scope 3 emissions are considered, the categorization into the 15 Scope 3 categories is not followed consistently. The specific application of activity-based methods in the context of Scope 3 accounting is exemplarily outlined by [10], mainly focusing on Category 1 (Purchased goods and services) and Category 2 (Capital goods). A more detailed discussion of the activity-based GHG measurement is provided in [13, 14] by introducing the 3-Levers of Emission Control (3-LoEC) framework. It offers a systematic approach for measuring GHG emissions by breaking down the emission-driving activities into production, power, and emission coefficients. This systematization enables an activity-based measurement of transportation (logistics) and production (manufacturing) processes. While activity-based accounting practices have begun to integrate sustainability issues and GHG emissions, there is still a lack of comprehensive integration across all 15 Scope 3 categories in sustainability accounting.

3 Integrated Cost and Scope 3 Accounting: Conceptualization

For integrated cost and GHG emissions accounting, the products created are the key reference point for calculating and forecasting further emissions and expenditure. Table 2, therefore, follows the integration of corporate and product carbon footprint according to the GHGP-Product-Standard. Due to the distinction between *attributable* and *non-attributable* processes [7], nine of the fifteen Scope 3 categories remain as an emission overhead. These categories have to be reported separately, as 'they do not become the product, make the product, or directly carry the product through its life cycle' [7, p. 135]. This leads to what Alvarez et al. [11] call the 'divergence problem'- the mismatch between product-level and organization-level carbon footprints and a remaining emission overhead. Hence, it is incorrect that the 'sum of all products and service carbon footprints is equal to the total carbon footprint of the associated organization [12]'.

Table 2. Life Cycle Stages and related Scope 1, 2 and 3-GHG emissions

Life Cycle Stage	Related Scope/Category (Cat.)
(I) Material acquisition and pre-processing	Cat. 1: Purchased Goods and Services Cat. 4: Upstream transportation and distribution
(II) Production	Scope 1 and Scope 2
(III) Distribution and Storage	Cat. 9: Downstream transportation and distribution
(IV) Use Phase	Cat. 10: Processing of the sold products Cat. 11: Use of sold products
(V) End-of-life treatment of the product	Cat. 12: End-of-life treatment of sold products
Remaining overhead	Cat. 2: Capital Goods Cat. 3: Fuel- and energy-related activities Cat. 5: Waste generated in operations Cat. 6: Business travel Cat. 7: Employee commuting Cat. 8: Upstream leased assets Cat. 13: Downstream leased assets Cat. 14: Franchises Cat. 15: Investments

This issue is similar to the overhead costing challenge described by Cooper & Kaplan [21], which led to the development of Activity-Based Costing (ABC). In traditional systems, overhead costs weren't directly traceable to products, resulting in inaccurate cost and pricing estimates. ABC solved this by allocating costs based on the actual resources used in production activities. For this reason, the proposed framework includes four key resource inputs: *Energy, Machinery and Equipment, Labor, Material and Services.*

These inputs are essential for production, and each incurs monetary costs. Aligning Scope 3-GHG emission categories with these resource inputs forms the basis of integrated activity-based cost & GHG accounting. However, this approach differs from the GHGP-Product-Standard, which maintains the distinction between *attributable* and *non-attributable* emissions. This difference is discussed further in Sect. 4.

Table 3 presents a systematic mapping of input resources to the relevant Scope 3 categories. Furthermore, exemplary assessment units are proposed that correspond to the units used in activity-based ERP system for product costing. Scope 3-GHG emissions can now be allocated via an additional attribute of an input resource, so that they are integrated with the cost accounting. When product costs are determined based on actual resource consumption, Scope 3-GHG emissions can be incorporated similarly. Furthermore, *Waste* can be seen as an output-resource, but the allocation of the costs for the waste treatment can be aligned with the corresponding Scope 3 Category 5 emissions in the same way as input resources. This alignment of costs and GHG emissions shows that all upstream emissions can be systematically included within an activity-based cost accounting framework.

Table 3. Categorization of resources and related Scope 1, 2 and 3-GHG emissions

Input-Resource	Related Scope/Category (Cat.)	Exemplary assessment units	
		Costing	GHG Emission
Material and Services	Cat. 1: Purchased goods and services Cat. 4: Upstream transportation and distribution	€/kg	Cat. 1 emission/kg Cat. 4 emission/ton-km
Energy	Scope 1 Scope 2 Cat. 3: Fuel- and energy-related activities	€/kWh	Scope 1/kWh Scope 2/kWh Cat. 3 emission/kWh
Machinery and Equipment	Cat. 2: Capital goods Cat. 8: Upstream leased assets	€/machinery hour	Cat. 2 emission/machine hour Cat. 8 emission/machine hour
Labor	Cat. 6: Business Travel Cat. 7: Employee commuting	€/working hour	Cat. 6 emission/working hour Cat. 7 emission/working hour
Output-Resource			
Waste	Cat. 5: Waste generation in operations	€/kg of waste	Cat. 5 emission/kg of waste

(*continued*)

Table 3. (*continued*)

Input-Resource	Related Scope/Category (Cat.)	Exemplary assessment units	
		Costing	GHG Emission
Finished Products	Cat. 9: Downstream transportation and distribution Cat. 10:Processing of sold products Cat. 11: Use of sold products Cat. 12: End-of-life treatment of sold products	Revenue €/Product	Cat. 9 emission/product Cat. 10 emission/product Cat. 11 emission/product Cat. 12 emission/product

The accounting of downstream emissions can follow a similar methodology: Categories 9 to 12 are connected to the further life cycle of the produced finished goods. Here, the revenue generated by the sales of the products can be used as a basis for assessment and for forecasting emissions. Following this concept, the emission overhead is reduced to Cat. 13: Downstream leased assets, Cat. 14: Franchises, and Cat. 15: Investments. These Scope 3 categories are difficult to be allocate to the product-centered accounting system, as the conceptual characteristics of the organization have a greater influence here. In the first instance, these Scope 3-GHG emissions occur independently of actual production within the company. Following this conceptualization, the 'divergence problem' is reduced to these remaining categories.

The integrated cost & Scope 3-GHG accounting system offers two key advantages: It can be used both for a historical analysis of costs and revenues, serving as a basis for emissions reporting, and for forecasting, to estimate future costs and emissions based on planned production and sales volumes. There are two key levers for improving environmental and cost performance: First, reducing resource input, for example, by increasing efficiency or using more resource-saving technologies. Second, changing the underlying activities outside of the organization, by contracting with better-performing partners [9] or substituting particularly emission-intensive operations. However, to identify the underlying activities, the inconsistency of the 15 Scope 3 categories is again a problem. While 9 of the 15 Scope 3 categories are already formulated as activities, the emissions of Categories 1 (Purchased Goods and Services), 2 (Capital goods), and 8 (Upstream leased assets) are each based on their respective production. Emissions are therefore not fixed but depend on the emission-driving activities of the equipment suppliers. As shown by [13], production and transportation activities can be examined more closely through activity-based emission measurement following the 3-LoEC-framework, allowing for a more detailed analysis of their resource use. In this context, information sharing across the value chain, for example, through IoT devices or cloud-based solutions [31] - can provide a more transparent and efficient way to track and calculate emissions, particularly in long-term partnerships with trusted business partners.

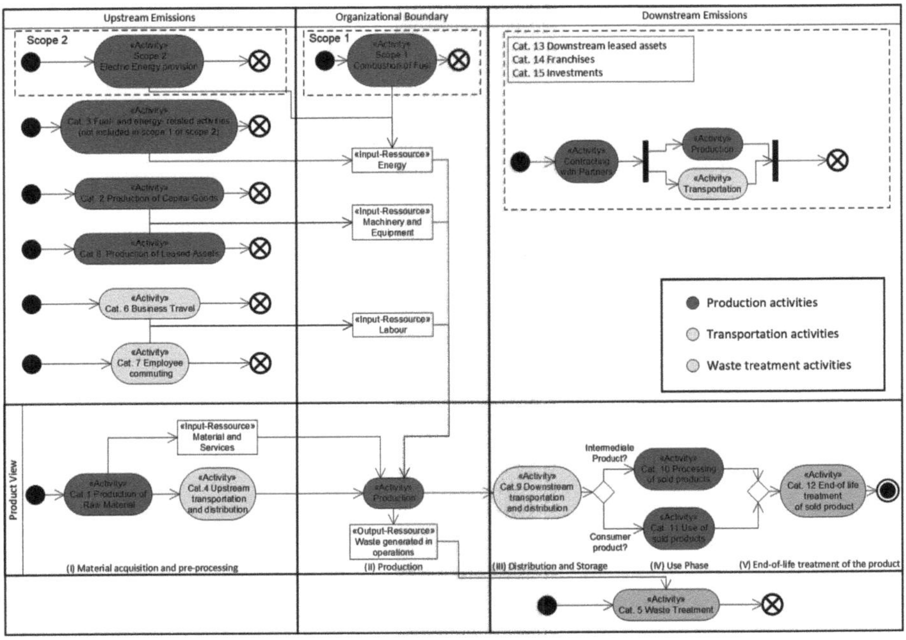

Fig. 1. Integrated Cost & Scope 3-GHG accounting system – UML-activity diagram

The UML-activity diagram presented in Fig. 1 provides an overview of the integrated perspective discussed before. The vertical swim lanes indicate where GHG emissions actually occur - either upstream, downstream, or within the organizational boundaries. As shown, all upstream emissions are through the usage of resources, all linked to the production process within the organizational boundaries. This consideration is important to understand Scope 3-GHG emissions not only as a reporting obligation, but also to become aware of the link to a company's own production.

Connecting resources and activities shows that all of the 15 Scope 3 categories are consistently related to production, transportation, or waste treatment activities. These activities can be further analysed using an activity-based GHG emission measurement approach to identify opportunities for reduction.

The horizontal swim lane represents the product CF perspective. It becomes evident that for product-level Scope 3-GHG reporting, only a significantly reduced portion of the actual emissions is considered, which highlights the gap between the full input resource related emissions and what is reported at the product level following the GHG-Product-Standard. It is argued that Categories 13 to 15 can be treated as a mixture of production, transportation, and waste treatment processes. However, it becomes clear that these activities lie outside the core logic of the actual production process and need to be further evaluated.

4 Integrated Cost and Scope 3 Accounting: Discussion

The conceptualization of an integrated activity-based Scope 3-GHG emission accounting revealed that the heterogeneity of the 15 Scope 3 categories, as well as the differentiation between *attributable* and *non-attributable* emissions, are the main problems that hinder the full integration of an activity-based cost and emission accounting system in compliance with the GHGP. From the perspective of cost accounting, the full integration of Scope 3 emissions (excluding the Category 13, Downstream leased assets, Category 14, Franchises, and Category 15, Investments) into an activity-based cost accounting system is useful to reveal the actual costs, the revenue, and their emissions accordingly. By using assessment units aligned with cost accounting, the actual GHG emissions appearing within the value chain can be traced back via the input resources needed in the production, transportation and waste treatment activities. However, to meet the requirements of both, i.e. the product CF reporting requirements and the requirement for internal decision-making and corporate CF reporting a 2-tiered accounting system is needed:

- The product-centered accounting system, which only includes *directly traced attributable* GHG emissions - those directly tied to the product life cycle (in line with the common GHGP-Product-Standard). The information provided by this system can be leveraged to better address customer demands in the further supply chain.
- The internal decision-making accounting system, which additionally includes *allocated non-attributable* GHG emissions, enables a more complete view of GHG emissions and cost drivers across the organization. Its provided information that can be used for the reporting of Scope 3-GHG emissions on a corporate level. By summing up the CF of all products and adding Categories 13–15, all Scope 1 and 2 as well as all Scope 3 categories are covered in that accounting system.

The 2-tiered accounting system allows for transparent *external reporting* while still supporting comprehensive *internal decision-making*. Regardless of the proposed conceptualization, data availability remains problematic. Refining activity-based measurements and investigating how the actual emissions arise in more detail, a company can improve the quality of the activity data and the results of the thereof related GHG accounting metrics.

From a legislative perspective, the heterogeneity of Scope 3-GHG emissions makes it difficult to form a comprehensive view of total GHG emissions. This raises the question of whether the current separation between corporate reporting and product reporting - reflected in the distinction between *attributable* and *non-attributable* emissions - remains meaningful. As is shown by the 2-tiered accounting system that underlies the integrated cost & Scope 3-GHG accounting a more transparent and consistent picture can be delivered by applying the activity-based accounting approach concerning the resources applied - both directly and indirectly - in the production, transportation and waste treatment activities and additionally allocating non-attributable emissions.

5 Conclusion

This paper proposes an integrated 2-tiered cost & Scope 3-GHG accounting system by linking the Greenhouse Gas Protocol (GHGP) framework with an activity-based cost accounting logic. By conceptualizing all 15 Scope 3 categories within a UML-activity diagram, this paper offers a foundation for aligning GHG emissions with their corresponding cost- and emission driving resources, thereby enabling more transparent, accurate, and actionable carbon footprint reporting.

The analysis reveals that Scope 3-GHG emissions, though occurring outside of organizational boundaries, are directly tied to production, transportation, and waste treatment processes. Through the integration of resource-based activity data - covering materials, energy, equipment, labor, and waste - these emissions can be effectively traced and allocated using principles derived from ABC. The 2-tiered accounting system enables the calculation of product and corporate-level GHG emissions in a harmonized way, improving both internal decision-making and external sustainability reporting.

Crucially, this approach also addresses the long-standing 'divergence problem' between product and corporate-level carbon footprints [11]. The two views in the 2-tiered accounting system - one focused on *directly traced attributable GHG emissions* for product-level reporting and another for comprehensive internal decision-making that also includes *allocated non-attributable GHG emissions* - bridge the gap between regulatory compliance and managerial relevance.

While data availability remains a challenge, especially in the early stages of implementation, an activity-based approach provides a clear path for improving emission data quality over time. Future research will focus on integrating the proposed framework into ERP systems to support dynamic GHG accounting that aligns with financial and operational planning. Ultimately, this paper advocates for a more holistic, transparent, and resource-based approach to Scope 3-GHG accounting - one that strengthens both regulatory compliance and sustainability performance across value chains.

References

1. Intergovernmental Panel on Climate Change (IPCC): Climate Change 2021 – The Physical Science Basis. Cambridge University Press (2023). https://doi.org/10.1017/9781009157896
2. Hettler, M., Graf-Vlachy, L.: Corporate scope 3 carbon emission reporting as an enabler of supply chain decarbonization: a systematic review and comprehensive research agenda. Bus Strategy Environ. (2023). https://doi.org/10.1002/bse.3486
3. EFRAG: Draft version ESRS E-1 (2022)
4. IFRS Foundation: IFRS - ISSB delivers further harmonisation of the sustainability disclosure landscape as it embarks on new work plan. https://www.ifrs.org/news-and-events/news/2024/06/issb-delivers-further-harmonisation-of-the-sustainability-disclosure-landscape-new-work-plan/. Accessed 27 Oct 2024
5. WBCSD; World Resource Institute: The Greenhouse Gas Protocol (2004)
6. WBCSD; World Resource Institute: Greenhouse Gas Protocol: Corporate Value Chain (Scope 3) Accounting and Reporting Standard (2011)
7. WBCSD; World Resource Institute: Greenhouse Gas Protocol: Product Life Cycle and Accounting Standard. (2011)

8. Klaaßen, L., Stoll, C.: Harmonizing corporate carbon footprints. Nat Commun. **12** (2021). https://doi.org/10.1038/s41467-021-26349-x
9. Kaplan, R.S., Ramanna, K.: We need better carbon accounting. Here's how to get there. Harv. Bus. Rev. Digit. Artic. (2022)
10. Kaplan, R.S., Ramanna, K.: Accounting for climate change. Harv Bus Rev., 1–21 (2021)
11. Alvarez, S., Carballo-Penela, A., Mateo-Mantecón, I., Rubio, A.: Strengths-weaknesses-opportunities-threats analysis of carbon footprint indicator and derived recommendations. J. Clean. Prod. **121**, 238–247 (2016). https://doi.org/10.1016/j.jclepro.2016.02.028
12. Damert, M., Morris, J., Guenther, E.: Carbon footprints of organizations and products, pp. 59–72 (2020). https://doi.org/10.1007/978-3-319-95726-5_12
13. Baumüller, J., Schwaiger, W., Typpelt, V.: Three levers of emission control (3-LoEC)-model: at the core of GHG emission-management control systems. In: 19th International Scientific Conference on Industrial Systems, pp. 412–419. Faculty of Technical Sciences (2023). https://doi.org/10.24867/IS-2023-T6.2-10_10041
14. Alaoui, L.H., Baumüller, J., Schwaiger, W.S.A.: 3-levers of emission control-modeling framework: modeling GHG emissions when direct measurement is not possible. In: International Sustainable Energy Conference – Proceedings, vol. 1 (2024). https://doi.org/10.52825/isec.v1i.1159
15. Wesumperuma, A., Ginige, A., Hol, A.: Green activity based reporting for organizational business process management (2015)
16. Stechemesser, K., Guenther, E.: Carbon accounting: a systematic literature review. J. Clean. Prod. **36**, 17–38 (2012). https://doi.org/10.1016/j.jclepro.2012.02.021
17. Wiedmann, T., Minx, J.: A definition of "carbon footprint" (2007)
18. Bjørn, A., Owsianiak, M., Molin, C., Hauschild, M.Z.: LCA history. In: Hauschild, M., Rosenbaum, R., Olsen, S. (eds.) Life Cycle Assessment, pp. 17–30. Springer, Cham (2018). https://doi.org/10.1007/978-3-319-56475-3_3
19. International Organization for Standardization: ISO 14040:2006 Environmental management - Life Cycle Assessment - Principles and framework (2006)
20. Leontief, W.: Input-Output Analysis. Oxford University Press, Oxford (1986)
21. Cooper, R., Kaplan, R.S.: Activity-based systems: measuring the costs of resource usage (1992)
22. Kaplan, R.S., Anderson, S.R.: Time-driven activity-based costing (2004)
23. Stuart, J.A., Turbini, L.J., Animons, J.C.: Activity-based environmental inventory allocation. J. Ind. Ecol. **2**, 95–108 (1998). https://doi.org/10.1162/jiec.1998.2.3.95
24. Emblemsvåg, J., Bras, B.: Activity-Based Cost and Environmental Management. Springer, New York (2001). https://doi.org/10.1007/978-1-4419-8604-7
25. Cagno, E., Micheli, G.J.L., Trucco, P.: Eco-efficiency for sustainable manufacturing: an extended environmental costing method. Prod. Plan. Control **23**, 134–144 (2012). https://doi.org/10.1080/09537287.2011.591628
26. Duran, O., Afonso, P.S.L.P.: An activity-based costing decision model for life cycle economic assessment in spare parts logistic management. Int. J. Prod. Econ. **222** (2020). https://doi.org/10.1016/j.ijpe.2019.09.020
27. Yang, C.H.: An optimization portfolio decision model of life cycle activity-based costing with carbon footprint constraints for hybrid green power strategies. Comput. Oper. Res. **96**, 256–271 (2018). https://doi.org/10.1016/j.cor.2018.03.003
28. Kayrbekova, D., Markeset, T., Ghodrati, B.: Activity-based life cycle cost analysis as an alternative to conventional LCC in engineering design. Int. J. Syst. Assur. Eng. Manag. **2**, 218–225 (2011). https://doi.org/10.1007/s13198-011-0064-7
29. Jourdaine, M., Loubet, P., Sonnemann, G., Trébucq, S.: The ABC-LCA method for the integration of activity-based costing and life cycle assessment. Bus Strategy Environ. **30**, 1735–1750 (2021). https://doi.org/10.1002/bse.2712

30. Sarkis, J., Meade, L., Presley, A.: An activity-based management methodology for evaluating business processes for environmental sustainability. Bus. Process. Manag. J. **12**, 751–769 (2006). https://doi.org/10.1108/14637150610710918
31. Rajkumar, D.M.N., Sruthi, M., Kumar, D.V.V.: IoT based smart system for controlling Co2 emission. Int. J. Sci. Res. Comput. Sci. Eng. Inf. Technol. **2**, 284 (2017)

Transforming Business with AI-Driven IoT Insights: Query, Process, and Visualize Data

Daniela Timisică[1,2(✉)], Răzvan-Alexandru Duţescu[1,2], and Radu Boncea[2]

[1] National University of Science and Technology POLITEHNICA Bucharest, Bucharest, Romania
[2] National Institute for Research and Development in Informatics - ICI Bucharest, Bucharest, Romania
daniela.timisica@ici.ro

Abstract. Integrating Artificial Intelligence (AI) with the Internet of Things (IoT) is revolutionizing business decision-making by enabling real-time intuitive access to complex sensor data. This paper presents an AI-powered assistant that allows enterprises to query, process, and visualize IoT-generated data through natural language interactions. Using large language models, automated analytics, and intelligent dashboards, the assistant streamlines the entire data pipeline - from data retrieval to predictive modeling - without requiring technical expertise. A case study demonstrates the assistant's application in monitoring energy consumption and temperature variations in multiple facilities, using a fusion-based IoT platform. The paper concludes by outlining future enhancements, including real-time streaming, multimodal interfaces, and domain-specific adaptation, positioning the assistant as a scalable and intelligent layer within enterprise IoT ecosystems.

Keywords: AI · IoT · Business Transformation · Data Processing · Visualization · Querying

1 Introduction

The convergence of Artificial Intelligence (AI) and the Internet of Things (IoT) redefines how businesses interact with data. As organizations adopt the digital infrastructure to monitor, control and optimize operations, IoT devices generate a continuous stream of structured and unstructured data. However, the sheer volume, velocity, and variability of IoT data present significant challenges for traditional data analysis approaches, which often require manual intervention, specialized technical expertise, and predefined query structures. These constraints hinder real-time decision making, limit data accessibility, and decrease responsiveness in dynamic business environments [2,4].

K. Wącel (Ed.): BIS 2025 Workshops, LNBIP 568, pp. 101–113, 2026.
https://doi.org/10.1007/978-3-032-11651-2_9

AI-driven technologies, particularly those using large language models (LLMs), machine learning (ML), and natural language processing (NLP), provide a transformative solution. They allow users to engage with complex data systems through intuitive, conversational interfaces that convert human queries into structured data operations. This evolution empowers both technical and non-technical stakeholders to extract actionable insights from the IoT data, decreasing reliance on specialized analysts and enhancing operational agility [5].

A key factor in this transformation is the integration of AI-powered assistants that can automate three essential tasks: querying data generated by the Internet of Things (IoT), processing the results to extract valuable patterns, and visualizing insights in a way that is accessible to business users. By automating these processes, organizations can reduce decision-making latency and improve workflows in various areas, such as energy management, supply chain logistics, innovative infrastructure, and predictive maintenance [3]. The AI assistant employs function-calling mechanisms and intelligent prompts to interact with the IoT platforms, providing structured analyses and dynamic dashboards with a minimal user input.

Additionally, this integration is in line with the wider trends of the digital transformation, where businesses aim to become more data-driven, responsive, and adaptable. The synergy between the AI and the IoT enables real-time monitoring, supports predictive analytics, and improves the scalability of the enterprise systems, all while making the user's experience simpler through natural language interfaces [1].

Business Contributions. This research makes four key business-oriented contributions:

1. An AI-powered querying mechanism that retrieves relevant IoT data using natural language inputs, removing the need for complex technical queries.
2. An AI-assisted data processing pipeline that transforms raw sensor data into actionable business intelligence through machine learning and statistical models.
3. An automated visualization module that converts analytical results into interactive dashboards, supporting the strategic decision-making.
4. A comprehensive business impact analysis that demonstrates how the AI-driven IoT integration enhances efficiency, improves decision-making and facilitates digital transformation in enterprise contexts.

This paper introduces an AI-powered assistant that exemplifies this paradigm shift. The proposed system enables businesses to query IoT data using natural language, automatically process the retrieved data through analytical pipelines, and visualize the results to support strategic decisions.

The paper is structured as follows: Sect. 2 reviews existing approaches to AI-driven querying, processing, and visualization of IoT data, highlighting current limitations in adaptability and flexibility. Section 3 introduces the system architecture and details the assistant's capabilities in querying IoT data, applying statistical and machine learning techniques, and generating business-relevant visualizations. Section 4 presents a practical enterprise case study, where energy and temperature data were retrieved from an IoT platform and analyzed to uncover correlations, forecast energy demand, and reduce operational costs. Section 5 examines the business impact of AI integration, emphasizing measurable improvements such as faster decision-making and cost optimization. Section 6 offers a quantitative evaluation of the assistant's performance, comparing its accuracy, responsiveness, and usability against traditional workflows, and discusses future development directions including real-time streaming, multimodal interaction, and explainability.

Through this work, we demonstrate how the AI can augment human interaction with the IoT ecosystems and significantly transform enterprise data workflows.

2 Related Work

Integrating Artificial Intelligence (AI) with the Internet of Things (IoT) has gained significant attention in academic and industrial contexts, driven by the need for intelligent data processing, adaptive querying, and responsive decision-making [6]). Early research in this domain focused on developing static rule-based systems to handle the IoT data, where predefined queries and rigid workflows dominated the analytics pipeline [8]. While effective in controlled environments, such systems lack the flexibility required in dynamic business operations, where data sources and decision criteria continuously evolve.

Researchers began exploring more adaptive frameworks for handling the IoT data as AI technologies advanced, particularly in machine learning (ML), natural language processing (NLP), and deep learning. For instance, [2] outlined an architecture emphasizing the need for scalable and intelligent data analytics to manage the deluge of information produced by the IoT networks. Their studies laid the groundwork for integrating the AI into the IoT workflows, recognizing that edge and cloud intelligence are essential for real-time responsiveness and business agility.

Recent studies have highlighted the transformative potential of large language models (LLMs) in their interactions with the IoT systems. LLMs allow users to express complex analytical requests in a natural language, which are then converted into structured queries that can be understood by backend IoT databases or APIs [5]. This capability reduces the technical barriers to accessing and analyzing data, enabling a broader organizational adoption and empowering non-technical business users to engage in data-driven decision-making. Additionally, the NLP-enhanced systems provide a level of semantic understanding and contextual reasoning that static dashboards cannot achieve [1].

The research in predictive analytics and smart infrastructure has highlighted the benefits of integrating the AI with the Internet of Things (IoT). Applications include anomaly detection in industrial systems [7], energy optimization in smart buildings [3], and real-time logistics management in supply chains [9]. These implementations demonstrate how the AI-driven systems can automate insights and adapt over time, improving with continuous data exposure and feedback.

Despite these advances, challenges still exist. Many AI-IoT systems operate in silos, lacking interoperability and the ability to synthesize diverse data sources. Concerns about explainability and transparency persist, especially when the AI-generated decisions impact critical business operations. The proposed research aims to address these issues by utilizing a modular architecture with transparent function-calling mechanisms, which will provide flexibility, extensibility, and foster user's trust.

3 Methodology

This paper introduces a meticulously designed modular AI-powered assistant, demonstrating how the AI can facilitate an intelligent interaction with the IoT data. The assistant is tailored to automate querying, processing, and visualization tasks within enterprise environments. The system architecture, grounded in a layered model, offers flexibility, extensibility, and seamless integration with the existing IoT platforms. The methodology is built on four main components: natural language querying, structured data retrieval, AI-based data processing, and automated visualization.

3.1 System Architecture

The AI assistant, acting as a powerful intermediary, empowers business users with its architecture consisting of the following core layers: input interpretation, query generation, data processing, and visualization output. Business users interact with the assistant using natural language prompts, made possible by the assistant's use of natural language processing (NLP) techniques. These techniques interpret prompts and translate them into structured queries compatible with the underlying IoT data sources.

Once the data are retrieved, they are processed using machine learning algorithms and statistical functions to extract actionable insights, enabling users to make informed decisions in real-time. Finally, the results are visualized using interactive tools, further empowering users with real-time decision support. This architecture allows for both cloud-based and edge computing deployment and supports scalable integration with APIs, time-series databases, and sensor fusion platforms. A diagram illustrating the architecture is provided in Fig. 1.

The Input Interpretation layer leverages an open-source Large Language Model (LLM), specifically SQL-LLaMa2, designed for efficient translation of natural language prompts into structured SQL queries and RESTful API calls. SQL-LLaMa2 interprets business user inputs by parsing the natural language request, identifying relevant entities and parameters, and automatically generating the corresponding structured queries compatible with the underlying IoT data sources, such as the OpenFuse IoT data-fusion platform.

The Data Processing layer integrates advanced analytical methods implemented via widely-used Python libraries. Time-series forecasting is handled by the ARIMA model using the statsmodels library. For anomaly detection, the

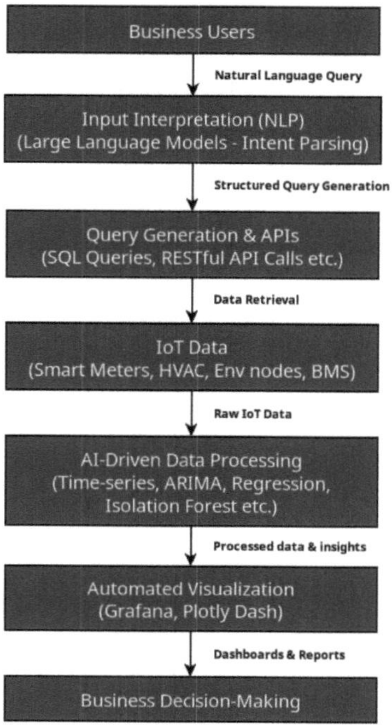

Fig. 1. AI-Powered IoT Business Analytics Framework.

Isolation Forest algorithm from scikit-learn is employed (with parameters such as n_estimators=100 and contamination=0.01). Additionally, linear regression analysis for identifying correlations (e.g., between temperature control settings and energy usage) is executed using scikit-learn.

Finally, the Visualization layer automatically generates interactive dashboards using Grafana and Plotly Dash. These visualizations provide real-time, actionable insights directly accessible to business users, significantly streamlining strategic decision-making.

3.2 Querying Business IoT Data

A distinguishing feature of the assistant is its user-friendly interface that translates natural language prompts into structured queries. This functionality is enabled through advanced LLMs such as SQL-LLaMa2 [10], a fine-tuned LLaMa-based model, which parses the semantics and intent of user input. For example, a prompt such as "Show me the energy consumption trends in our facilities over the last month" is interpreted contextually and converted into an SQL. The aforementioned prompt would output the following SQL query:

```
SELECT
    facility_name,
   DATE_TRUNC('day', reading_date) AS day,
```

```
    SUM(usage_kwh) AS total_kwh
FROM energy_usage
WHERE reading_date >= CURRENT_DATE - INTERVAL '30days'
GROUP BY facility_name, day
ORDER BY facility_name, day;
```

This transformation leverages schema-aware prompting and context-driven mapping between user input and database structures. The assistant is able to dynamically infer temporal ranges, aggregation functions, and grouping keys directly from the phrasing of the user's request.

Table 1. Comparison of Traditional vs. AI-Powered IoT Querying

Features	Traditional Querying	AI-Powered Querying
Query Format	Structured syntax such as SQL or predefined API calls	Natural Language prompts interpreted via NLP
Flexibility	Low – limited to predefined queries and static interfaces	High – dynamically generates queries based on context
User Expertise	High – requires technical knowl-edge and query-building skills	Low – accessible to non-technical users
Adaptabillity	Limited – difficult to adjust to changing business needs	Adaptive – can respond to varied and evolving business scenarios
Processing Time	Slower – often involves manual configuration and revisions	Faster – automated query generation and execution
Scalability	Constrained – requires individual query design per use case	Scalable – reusable across domains with minimal reconfiguration

Unlike traditional querying methods, which typically require users to compose or select predefined SQL statements manually, the proposed approach enables adaptive and context-sensitive query generation. To illustrate these benefits, Table 1 compares traditional versus AI-powered IoT querying in terms of query format, flexibility, required expertise, and processing time.

To further evaluate the effectiveness of the generated SQL queries, we conducted experiments with 30 natural language prompts across three representative database schemas (energy usage, HVAC, and environmental data). SQL-LLaMA2 achieved a correctness rate of 86%, as measured against manually validated ground-truth queries. The most common errors involved misapplied aggregation functions or missing join conditions, both of which were easily resolved with minimal user intervention.

3.3 Business Data Processing

Once the relevant data is retrieved, they undergo automated processing. The assistant applies statistical analyses and machine learning techniques to extract patterns, detect anomalies, and perform forecasting. Core techniques include time-series analysis, clustering, and regression-based modeling, which help identify trends and correlations in business operations. These models are executed through predefined function-calling mechanisms, allowing the assistant to dynamically invoke relevant processing tools based on the user's query context.

This step accelerates the insight generation process and minimizes human bias in interpreting raw data. The assistant's modular design also allows developers to incorporate domain-specific models, enhancing customization for specific business sectors.

Once the IoT data is retrieved, it undergoes automated analytical processing using statistical methods and machine learning algorithms implemented through predefined Python libraries. Specifically:

1. Time-series analysis is conducted using the ARIMA (AutoRegressive Integrated Moving Average) model, as implemented in Python's statsmodels library (e.g., ARIMA(2,1,2)). This technique is essential for accurately forecasting future energy consumption trends.
2. Anomaly detection leverages the Isolation Forest algorithm from the scikit-learn library, configured with typical parameters (n_estimators=100, contamination=0.01). This method efficiently detects unusual spikes or deviations in energy usage and temperature data, which could indicate inefficiencies or faults.
3. Linear regression analysis, also executed via scikit-learn, is employed to identify and quantify correlations between key variables such as HVAC temperature controls and corresponding energy consumption. This regression modeling facilitates predictive insights and operational optimization.

3.4 Business Data Visualization

The final component of the assistant's pipeline is the automatic generation of visualizations. After processing the data, the assistant selects the most appropriate chart type and visualization method based on the nature of the dataset and the user's intent. Matplotlib, Plotly, and Grafana are used to create real-time dashboards and interactive graphs.

Visualizations are designed to support strategic business decision-making, enabling users to grasp performance metrics quickly, detect anomalies, or forecast operational changes. This capability reduces manual data reporting and allows for continuous monitoring of enterprise systems.

4 Case Study and Business Evaluation: Energy Consumption Analysis with AI Assistant

4.1 Scenario Overview

This case study illustrates the practical application of the proposed AI assistant in analyzing energy consumption and temperature variation across multiple enterprise facilities. The enterprise utilizes a fusion-based IoT platform that consolidates real-time data from smart meters, HVAC systems, external weather nodes, and Building Management Systems (BMS). The objective is to identify energy inefficiencies, forecast consumption trends, and enable data-driven optimization decisions.

4.2 Data Sources and Query Execution

The AI assistant operates on data integrated via OpenFuse, a middleware platform that standardizes time-series IoT data and offers RESTful APIs. The main data sources include:

1. Smart Meters (for granular energy usage)
2. HVAC Sensors (monitoring internal climate conditions)
3. Environmental IoT nodes (external temperature and humidity)
4. Building Management Systems (BMS)

A business user can simply issue a prompt such as: "Show me energy and temperature trends across all departments for the last 30 days.".

The assistant, powered by SQL-LLaMa2, interprets the user's intent, extracts key entities (departments, metrics, time range), and generates the following structured API request:

```
GET /api/v1/departments/all/energy-temp?range=last_30_days
```

This request is submitted to the OpenFuse platform, which responds with structured sensor data. To enable correct API call generation, the assistant was provided with the OpenFuse schema and OpenAPI specifications, which describe the available endpoints, parameters, and data types. This schema-awareness was injected into the prompting process, ensuring that SQL-LLaMA2 could correctly align user intent with the expected API contract. In cases where schema metadata was omitted, the correctness of generated API calls dropped significantly (to around 58%), underscoring the importance of supplying the model with explicit API documentation. The assistant handles all necessary preprocessing steps, including timestamp alignment, unit normalization (e.g., ° C, kWh), and interpolation of missing values, ensuring that the data is analysis-ready.

The processed data is then automatically visualized through integrated Grafana dashboards. For example, Fig. 2 illustrates a system-generated trend graph showing energy consumption and temperature fluctuations, with anomaly indicators clearly marked for facility managers.

4.3 Automated Data Processing

Once the data is retrieved, the assistant applies several machine learning and statistical techniques:

1. Descriptive statistics: average energy use per department, standard deviation, and percentile distribution.

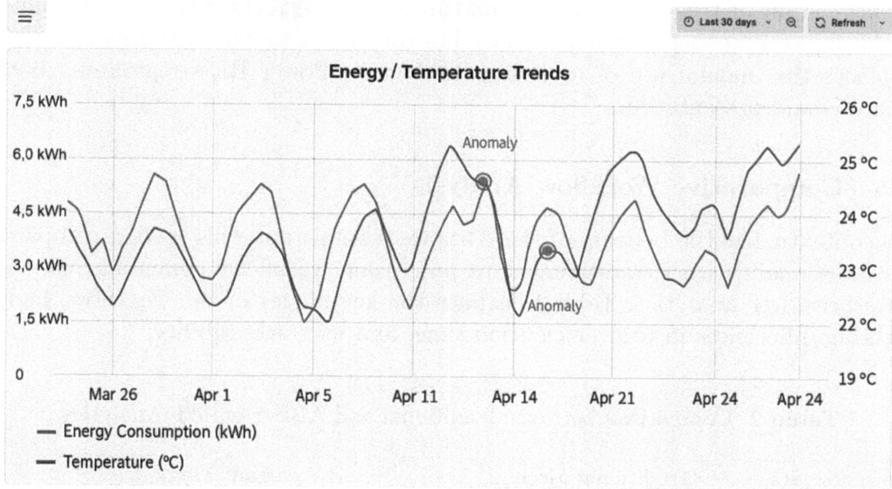

Fig. 2. Dashboard example visualizing energy and temperature trends along with detected anomalies.

2. Anomaly detection: the Isolation Forest model (n_estimators=100, contamination=0.01) indicates unusual spikes or temperature inconsistencies.
3. Predictive analytics:
   1. ARIMA models forecast short-term energy demand with high accuracy.
   2. Linear Regression is applied to correlate temperature control vs energy efficiency
   3. Clustering (K-Means) identifies usage patterns by zone (e.g., office vs warehouse).

These steps are triggered dynamically using predefined Python functions based on the context of the user prompt. Compared to traditional workflows requiring multiple analysts and hours of coordination, the assistant performs all processing in under 15 s.

4.4 Visualization and Dashboard Generation

The assistant automatically generates visual insights using Plotly Dash and Grafana:

1. Trend graphs: quarter-wise energy usage with forecast overlays
2. Heatmaps: hourly temperature fluctuations across zones
3. Anomaly timelines: visual identification of irregular usage

Dashboards are interactive, automatically generated using Grafana and Plotly Dash, providing intuitive, user-friendly interfaces that facilitate quick identification of trends, anomalies, and insights. Users can apply filters (time, location, equipment) and export insights directly into business reports. This replaces the manual use of tools like Tableau or Power BI, streamlining both analysis and presentation.

4.5 Comparative Workflow Analysis

To contextualize the benefits of the AI-powered assistant, this section compares its functionality with traditional data processing workflows commonly used in enterprise IoT analytics. Table 2 outlines the key stages of the workflow, highlighting differences in tools, execution time, and user accessibility.

Table 2. Comparison between Traditional and AI-Driven IoT Analytics

Workflow Stage	Traditional Method	AI Assistant Method
Data Querying	Manual SQL or API queries crafted by technical teams	Natural language prompts interpreted by SQL-LLaMa2
Data Preprocessing	Custom scripts for normalization and handling missing values	Automated preprocessing, including unit alignment and smoothing
Analytical Modeling	Manual model selection and implementation (e.g., Python, R)	ARIMA, regression, and clustering triggered automatically
Visualization	Requires BI tools, separate design of dashboards	Auto-generated via Grafana and Plotly Dash, eliminating the need for external BI tools
Turnaround Time	Several hours to days	Seconds to minutes
Required Expertise	High – data scientists and IT professionals	Low – accessible to business users with no coding knowledge
Adaptability	Low – queries and dashboards must be manually adjusted	High – dynamically adapts to diverse prompts and business contexts
Insight Delivery	Delayed – insights depend on reporting cycles and analyst schedules	Immediate – insights delivered within the interaction session

The AI assistant significantly reduces complexity by integrating all core stages—querying, processing, modeling, and visualization—into a unified conversational interface. Traditional pipelines involve multiple tools, manual effort, and specialized skills, often resulting in delays and fragmented insights.

In contrast, the assistant streamlines access to actionable analytics, shortens feedback loops, and democratizes data interaction across departments. By eliminating the dependency on specialized personnel, it empowers domain experts and decision-makers to explore trends and anomalies directly, accelerating operational responses.

This comparison highlights not only the technical automation achieved through the assistant but also its potential to reshape organizational workflows and foster a more agile, data-informed culture.

4.6 Business Outcomes and Impact

The assistant revealed a strong correlation ($R^2 = 0.76$) between HVAC anomalies and sudden energy spikes. Forecasts generated by ARIMA models showed a mean absolute percentage error (MAPE) of less than 8.3%, enabling accurate short-term energy planning. Following anomaly corrections based on assistant recommendations, the enterprise observed a 4.7% reduction in energy costs over one month.

Beyond technical efficiency, the assistant enhanced business agility by delivering insights in real-time, eliminating delays from reporting cycles. Its conversational interface empowered managers and analysts alike to engage directly with complex sensor data without relying on technical teams.

5 Results and Discussion

Following the implementation and integration of the AI assistant within the enterprise IoT environment, multiple performance indicators were evaluated: query interpretation accuracy, forecasting reliability, usability, and overall responsiveness compared to traditional workflows.

The assistant consistently demonstrated high reliability in interpreting natural language queries. Using SQL-LLaMa2, it generated valid API calls with minimal error, adapting effectively to different formulations and time frames. Users were able to retrieve contextualized data with no technical knowledge of query languages or APIs.

In terms of forecasting, ARIMA models achieved a MAPE below 8.3%, providing sufficient accuracy for short-term energy demand planning. Linear regression yielded a strong R^2 score of 0.76, confirming a measurable correlation between HVAC behavior and consumption spikes. These results validate the assistant's analytical modules as both accurate and actionable in real business scenarios.

From a usability perspective, the assistant enabled non-technical users to explore and visualize data in under 15 s, compared to hours or days using traditional tools. The conversational interface and built-in Grafana integration allowed for dynamic, interactive dashboards, facilitating rapid operational responses.

Overall, the AI-powered assistant transforms enterprise IoT analytics into a streamlined, accessible, and adaptive process. It reduces dependency on technical personnel, accelerates insight delivery, and supports data-driven decision-making across departments.

6 Conclusion and Future Work

This paper presented an AI-powered assistant designed to transform how enterprises interact with IoT data by enabling natural language querying, automated processing, and real-time visualization. By combining natural language processing (NLP), machine learning (ML), and dynamic dashboards, the assistant enables non-technical users to query, analyze, and interpret complex sensor data effectively and intuitively.

The system, built upon the open-source SQL-LLaMA2 model, bridges the gap between business users and IoT platforms through an accessible conversational interface. A real-world case study focused on monitoring energy consumption and temperature variations across enterprise facilities demonstrated the assistant's ability to translate natural language prompts into structured queries, retrieve and process time-series data, and apply predictive analytics such as ARIMA forecasting and Isolation Forest anomaly detection. Within seconds, the assistant generated actionable visualizations via Grafana, significantly reducing the effort, delays, and expertise typically required in traditional workflows.

The evaluation confirmed both technical and business value: forecasting accuracy with MAPE below 8.3%, a strong correlation ($R^2 = 0.76$) between HVAC anomalies and energy spikes, and a 4.7% reduction in energy costs over a one-month period. These results validate the assistant's analytical robustness and demonstrate its capacity to deliver immediate, data-driven insights without requiring programming skills or specialized tools.

Positioned at the intersection of AI and IoT, the assistant contributes to broader digital transformation efforts by enabling scalable, flexible, and intuitive data interactions within enterprise environments.

6.1 Future Work

While the current implementation has demonstrated significant promise, several avenues for a future enhancement have been identified:

1. Security and Compliance: Strengthening data protection through encryption, access control, and compliance with enterprise security policies.
2. Real-Time Streaming Integration: Extending capabilities to handle live sensor data streams for proactive monitoring and instant anomaly detection.
3. Multimodal Interaction: Adding voice input, visual recognition, or gesture-based commands to broaden accessibility and improve usability across roles and devices.
4. Domain-Specific Adaptation: Training the assistant on vertical-specific datasets and terminology (e.g., logistics, healthcare, retail) to increase contextual relevance and analytical precision.
5. Explainability and Feedback Loops: Incorporating interpretable AI models and user's feedback mechanisms to continuously refine query understanding, output accuracy, and trust in recommendations.

With these enhancements, the assistant is positioned to evolve into a foundational layer of enterprise intelligence—capable not only of interpreting IoT data but also of adapting dynamically to evolving user needs, compliance requirements, and technological infrastructures.

AI Usage Declaration. Parts of this work involved the use of Large Language Models (LLMs), specifically SQL-LLaMA2, for generating and testing natural language to SQL translations. The model outputs were validated manually by the authors to ensure correctness. No generative AI tools were used for the writing or editing of this manuscript.

Acknowledgement. The authors acknowledge the support of project PN 23 38 01 01, "Contributions to the consolidation of emerging technologies specific to the Internet of Things and complex systems", which provided technical resources essential to this research.

References

1. Cheng, Y., Yang, Y., Zhang, W., Guo, Y.: AI-driven approaches for business intelligence in IoT-enabled environments. J. Ind. Inf. Integr. **27**, 100293 (2022)
2. Gubbi, J., Buyya, R., Marusic, S., Palaniswami, M.: Internet of Things (IoT): a vision, architectural elements, and future directions. Futur. Gener. Comput. Syst. **29**(7), 1645–1660 (2013)
3. Li, S., Da Xu, L., Zhao, S.: The internet of things: a survey. Inf. Syst. Front. **17**(2), 243–259 (2020)
4. Manyika, J., et al.: Big Data: The Next Frontier for Innovation, Competition, and Productivity. McKinsey Global Institute (2015). https://www.mckinsey.com/business-functions/mckinsey-digital/our-insights/big-data-the-next-frontier-for-innovation
5. Zhang, C., Zhao, Z., Xu, X., Wang, Y.: AIoT: When artificial intelligence meets the internet of things. J. Phys: Conf. Ser. **1881**(4), 042088 (2021)
6. Eventus.: Introduction to SEKHMET: Revolutionizing Data Processing with AIoT (2025). https://sekhmet.tech/features/aiot
7. Al-Turjman, F., Ever, E., Zahmatkesh, H.: Small-scale healthcare-related IoT-based systems: an overview. IEEE Syst. J. **12**(3), 3126–3137 (2018)
8. Perera, C., Zaslavsky, A., Christen, P., Georgakopoulos, D.: Context aware computing for the internet of things: a survey. IEEE Commun. Surv. Tutorials **16**(1), 414–454 (2014)
9. Zhou, K., Fu, C., Yang, S.: Big data driven smart energy management: from big data to big insights. Renew. Sustain. Energy Rev. **56**, 215–225 (2020)
10. Lindorfer, D.: SQL-LLaMA: Text-2-SQL using an Instruction-following LLaMA-2 Model [Computer software]. GitHub (2023). https://github.com/DominikLindorfer/SQL-LLaMA2

Integrating Data Science in Decision Support Systems for Risk Management: An Application in Human Trafficking Risk Assessment

Monica-Teodora Scăunaşu(✉)

Computer Science Department, National University of Science and Technology POLITEHNICA Bucharest, Bucharest, Romania
monica.scaunasu@stud.acs.upb.ro

Abstract. This paper presents a DSS for human trafficking risk assessment, combining machine learning with socio-legal indicators defined by Romanian Law 678/2001 and the MNIR framework. The system combines a Random Forest classifier with socio-demographic indicators to produce case-level risk profiling and explainable outputs. By incorporating MNIR-based scoring alongside machine learning predictions, the DSS ensures both predictive accuracy and alignment with established legal frameworks. Transparency is achieved through SHAP-based feature attribution, fairness through the integration of contextual factors, and traceability through the storage of predictions in a structured database. The prototype demonstrates how AI can support timely and human-centered risk management in organizational and legal contexts.

Keywords: Risk Management · Data Science · Decision Support System (DSS) · Human Trafficking · Predictive Modeling

1 Introduction

The risks may include those of a business that have effects on operations, finances, and reputation. Conservative risk management tools are insufficient today, as there are new demanding circumstances. Increasing risk complexity according to technological, global, and regulatory changes has been pointed out by Schroeck et al. [1].

They suggest combining different risk management strategies to harmonize such pressures. Traditional risk management (TRM) often focuses narrowly on departmental or isolated categories of risk, overlooking cross-functional interdependencies and emerging phenomena. Such outdated approaches tend to respond weakly to dynamic threats, whereas predictive analytics and machine learning enable proactive detection and mitigation of risks [2,3].

Data science identifies patterns in structured data (e.g., demographic records like age, gender, and country of origin) and unstructured data (e.g., victim statements or NGO case files), facilitating early identification of human trafficking

K. Wącel (Ed.): BIS 2025 Workshops, LNBIP 568, pp. 114–126, 2026.
https://doi.org/10.1007/978-3-032-11651-2_10

risks. For instance, clustering techniques can reveal recurrent routes or recruiter profiles, while natural language processing can detect indicators of coercion in textual reports.

With the combination of Decision Support Systems (DSS), it assists decision-makers to analyze the data and make real-time decisions.

This paper investigates how DSS and data science improve risk assessment, emphasizing explainable AI techniques, such as SHAP, for individual-level human trafficking risk profiling.

2 State of the Art: Data Science and Decision Support Systems in Risk Management

2.1 Difficulties in Traditional Risk Management (TRM)

Traditional risk management (TRM) has long been the foundation of organizational risk governance. However, its relevance has been questioned in light of increasingly complex and dynamic threats. As noted by Tohidi [4], risk management should shift from reactive, compartmentalized practices toward proactive, business-process-centered approaches supported by adaptable technology.

The limitations of TRM can be grouped into four main categories, each with notable levels of impact on organizational resilience:

1. Siloed Approach to Risk Management (Impact: Medium to High). When risks are addressed in isolation by different departments, organizations fail to perceive systemic vulnerabilities. Suarez [5] emphasizes that this lack of integration increases exposure to breakdowns and information loss. DSS platforms combined with data science can consolidate multi-source data, enabling cross-functional visibility and collaborative mitigation.
2. Poor Incorporation of Technology (Impact: Medium to High). Many organizations continue to rely on spreadsheets and rule-based systems that are inadequate for data-intensive environments. Tan et al. [6] highlight resource limitations as a barrier to modern analytics adoption. Embedding data science methods in DSS—using tools like Python, R, or automated ETL processes—can introduce real-time analytics and AI insights accessible even to non-specialists. Brynjolfsson and McAfee [7] further argue that the economic benefits of AI adoption can outweigh initial technological barriers, encouraging organizations to transition from traditional tools to advanced DSS.
3. Compliance-Based Rather than Strategic Orientation (Impact: Low to Medium). Jordan & Mitchell [8] note that machine learning innovations can enhance compliance processes, thereby fostering resilience, a perspective complemented by Agrawal et al. [9] who explore the economic implications of AI in strategic decision-making. TRM often emphasizes control and documentation at the expense of foresight. By contrast, DSS augmented with data science techniques such as decision trees, SHAP analysis, or optimization models help organizations reconcile compliance requirements with strategic objectives.

4. Over-Reliance on Past Data (Impact: Medium to High). Classical risk assessment presupposes that future risks mirror past events, which is unsuitable in fast-changing environments. Culp et al. [10] underline that models based solely on historical data quickly lose relevance, emphasizing the need for dynamic risk management strategies as outlined by Hardy [11] for government professionals to adapt to evolving threats. In contrast, scenario simulations and predictive analytics supported by data science offer forward-looking perspectives. Integrated DSS can detect emerging risks such as cyber vulnerabilities or social exploitation trends.

2.2 Overlaps Between Data Science and Decision Support Systems (DSS)

Data science integrated with DSS supports proactive risk management, as evidenced by predictive models for fraud detection, supply chain optimization, and public health early-warning systems. In the context of human trafficking, such integration allows the identification of high-risk migration routes, detection of recruitment patterns, and estimation of individual vulnerability scores before exploitation occurs.

Data science contributes predictive modeling, anomaly detection, and interpretability tools, while DSS provide the organizational infrastructure to embed these methods into decision processes [12,13].

Machine learning and real-time data processing have enabled risk governance to anticipate and respond to threats in ways traditional methods could not [14]. For example, anomaly detection techniques can uncover unseen patterns of fraud or irregularities in financial systems [14,15]. Predictive analytics using time-series forecasting help identify potential market downturns [13,16], while ensemble methods such as random forests provide robust insights into credit risk and loan default probabilities [17].

At the same time, DSS platforms transform these analytical outputs into actionable knowledge. Through dashboards, visualization tools, and scenario simulators, DSS allow managers to compare options and weigh trade-offs under uncertainty. In finance, DSS track credit portfolios and manage exposure [16]; in supply chains, they identify bottlenecks and propose real-time solutions [13]; in cybersecurity, they support detection and rapid response to intrusions [18].

Explainable AI (XAI) tools such as SHAP [19] and LIME [20] further strengthen this overlap. They make the outputs of complex models transparent and trustworthy, fostering acceptance among decision-makers and regulators. In this sense, DSS act as translators: they connect the technical strengths of data science with the practical requirements of strategic decision making.

Data science and DSS are complementary: data science provides predictive capacity, DSS ensures integration and governance. Together, they enhance organizational resilience and create adaptive, evidence-based risk management systems [4,16,21]. Moreover, Altman and Sabato [22] provide insights into credit risk modeling that can be integrated into DSS, while Turban et al. [23] highlight the role of business intelligence systems in enhancing decision-making processes.

2.3 Risk Response Types in Data-Driven DSS

Risk responses have traditionally been classified into four categories: avoidance, reduction, transfer, and acceptance. While the taxonomy remains unchanged, the integration of data science into DSS significantly enhances their precision and adaptability.

1. **Avoidance:** Risks can be preemptively eliminated when DSS forecast high-risk scenarios. For instance, predictive models can anticipate financial market volatility, allowing firms to avoid high-exposure investments [13,24]. DSS also simulate supply chain risks, supporting redesigns before critical disruptions occur.
2. **Reduction:** Data-driven DSS enable real-time risk mitigation. In cybersecurity, anomaly detection allows organizations to intercept threats as they arise [18,25]. In insurance, decision tree models assist in identifying fraudulent claims, thereby reducing exposure [15].
3. **Transfer:** Organizations often transfer risks via insurance or outsourcing. DSS simplify such decisions by comparing cost–benefit ratios and analyzing coverage gaps. Predictive models further refine the valuation of hazards, enabling more informed negotiations with third parties [16].
4. **Acceptance:** Certain risks cannot be economically mitigated and must be consciously accepted. DSS provide probabilistic impact assessments that support informed acceptance. For instance, startups may decide to enter new markets despite uncertainty, based on quantified assessments of risk and potential return [14].

What distinguishes modern DSS from classical approaches is their dynamic character: through explainable, data-driven analytics, they convert static frameworks into adaptive strategies that evolve with the environment [12,13,26].

2.4 Advantages, Challenges, and Implications for Risk Management

The literature demonstrates that while TRM provides a starting point, its weaknesses—fragmentation, outdated tools, compliance-driven focus, and reliance on historical data—limit its effectiveness. Data science addresses these gaps by introducing predictive power, anomaly detection, and interpretability. DSS serve as the organizational medium where these methods can be embedded into structured, transparent, and actionable processes.

Furthermore, the integration of data science and DSS brings notable advantages. Risk management becomes faster, more precise, and evidence-based, reducing human error and enabling real-time detection in domains such as finance and cybersecurity [26]. Scalability allows organizations to manage rising data volumes without sacrificing performance [27]. Visualization and simulation capabilities support anticipation of supply chain failures and corrective action [14].

However, the literature also cautions against significant challenges. Data quality and accessibility issues may compromise model reliability [28], as Batini and Scannapieco [28] provide a comprehensive framework for ensuring data integrity, a critical factor in risk modeling. Complex AI models can lack interpretability, creating concerns of transparency and regulation [29], as Lipton [29] discusses the mythos surrounding model interpretability, while Lazer et al. [30] highlight broader big data pitfalls that impact analytical trust. Ethical challenges such as algorithmic bias and autonomous decision-making must be carefully managed [31], with Mittelstadt et al. [32] providing a comprehensive mapping of ethical debates in AI, emphasizing the need for transparency and fairness in automated systems to address societal impacts.

Finally, resistance to change within organizations can slow adoption, requiring strong leadership support [33], as Kotter [33] emphasizes the importance of effective change management, a principle also relevant to integrating new DSS technologies.

Integrating data science into DSS reframes risk management as a continuous, adaptive practice capable of addressing uncertainty in real time, moving beyond static checklists toward evidence-based processes that strengthen resilience and innovation [12–14].

3 A Prototype Decision Support System for Victim-Level Human Trafficking Risk Profiling Using Machine Learning

3.1 Design Decisions

The prototype DSS introduces a supervised machine learning pipeline for exploitation risk assessment at the victim level. Unlike general-purpose monitoring tools, which concentrate on migration flows or criminal networks, this system provides individualized predictions based on legally defined social and demographic risk factors.

The data used in this prototype originate from the Romanian National Agency Against Human Trafficking (ANITP) [34], covering the period 2015–2023. The dataset includes approximately 1,200 records, with sexual exploitation representing about 60% of cases. Variables considered include age, gender, education, relationship with recruiter, and dwelling environment. All cases were anonymized to comply with GDPR regulations.

In line with Romanian Law 678/2001 and the National Identification and Referral Mechanism (MNIR), the system was developed in Python, using a Streamlit interface. A Random Forest classifier was selected because it performed better than logistic regression, particularly in predicting minority classes. The model achieved a cross-validation accuracy of 0.62 (SD = 0.19) and a weighted F1-score of 0.96 on the test set, confirming its strong predictive performance in spite of class imbalance. Interpretability is provided through SHAP (Shapley Additive Explanations), which helps identify the influence of features such as gender, education, or recruiter relationship. However, the multi-class SHAP visualization still requires refinement.

3.2 System Architecture

The DSS is organized around three main components. The first is the data layer, which involves the collection and preprocessing of ANITP case-level data [34] so that they can be used in machine learning tasks. The second is the model layer, where the Random Forest classifier operates on anonymized records to generate probabilistic predictions of exploitation type. The third is the interface layer, which provides a user-friendly Streamlit application that allows practitioners to enter victim characteristics and receive transparent, ranked predictions.

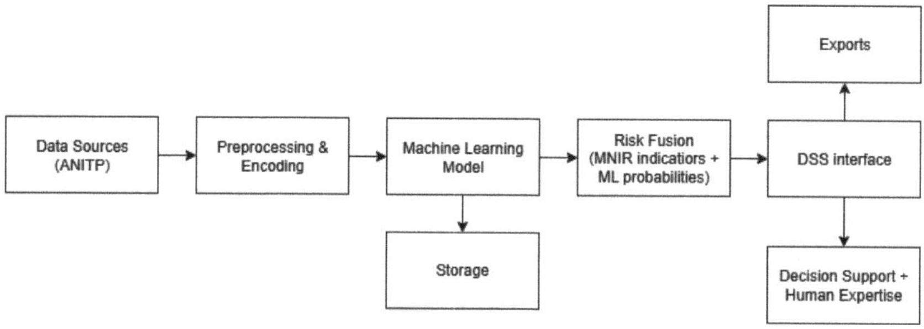

Fig. 1. System architecture of the proposed DSS for human trafficking risk assessment

Figure 1 illustrates the architecture of the proposed Decision Support System (DSS). Data from ANITP [34] are preprocessed and encoded, then passed through the machine learning model. Predictions are stored for traceability and combined with MNIR indicators in the risk fusion layer. The DSS interface presents the results to end-users, offering both exports (PNG, PDF, CSV) for reporting and structured decision support in combination with human expertise.

Unlike international platforms such as Polaris [35], Frontex [36], or IOM [37], which focus on aggregate monitoring and cross-border coordination, the proposed DSS architecture is tailored for local, case-level triage and decision support in line with national legal standards. At the same time, its modular design ensures that legal and social indicators can be directly linked with predictive analytics, while supporting scalability and future integration with institutional workflows.

3.3 Functional and Analytical Evaluation

The DSS provides a probabilistic distribution of possible exploitation outcomes for each victim case, as illustrated in Table 1. As an example, this corresponds to an individual characterized as follows: female, destination country Germany, Romanian citizenship, rural origin environment, county of residence Vaslui, education level 9–12 classes, recruiter identified as life partner, and age 19 years.

On the computer output, predictions are ordered, which allows the user to investigate both primary and secondary risks, as well as model uncertainty. For

Table 1. Predicted Probabilities of Exploitation Types (Case-Level Example)

ID	Exploitation Type	Probability (%)
0	Sexual Exploitation	70
1	Attempted Exploitation	17
2	Sexual (ambiguous label)	9
3	Forced Begging	2
4	Labor Exploitation	1
5	Begging	1
6	Theft	0
7	Other Exploitation Situations	0
8	Other Situations	0
9	Work (similar to Labor Exploitation)	0
10	Forced Theft	0
11	Forced to Commit Thefts or Other Offenses	0
12	Forced to Commit Crimes	0
13	Attempts at Any Kind of Exploitation	0

instance, in this case, the system indicated a 70% likelihood of sexual exploitation, 17% for attempted exploitation, and 9% for the duplicate label "sexual." This ranked approach improves transparency and supports human-in-the-loop decision-making.

Such overlaps in labels, like Sexual Exploitation versus Sexual or Forced Begging versus Begging, reflect inconsistencies in the dataset. Future work will focus on harmonizing categories to ensure consistency and improve the reliability of decision support outputs.

The mean predictive accuracy over 5-fold cross-validation was 0.62 with a standard deviation of 0.19. While modest in absolute terms, this result is relatively high in the context of multi-class classification tasks in social risk detection. Cross-validation also prevents overfitting, ensuring that the model generalizes well to unseen cases.

The classification report indicates a global F1-score of 0.96. Minority classes, such as forced theft or forced participation in crimes, showed lower recall because of their rarity, yet their inclusion illustrates the comprehensive scope of the DSS (see Fig. 2).

Decision logic is exemplified by combining model outputs with MNIR-based indicators. For example, when sexual exploitation was predicted with 70% probability and the MNIR score was 4 out of 10, the case was classified as moderate risk, leading to a recommendation for monitoring and counseling. This hybrid approach ensures congruence between predictive outputs and legal–social requirements (see Fig. 3).

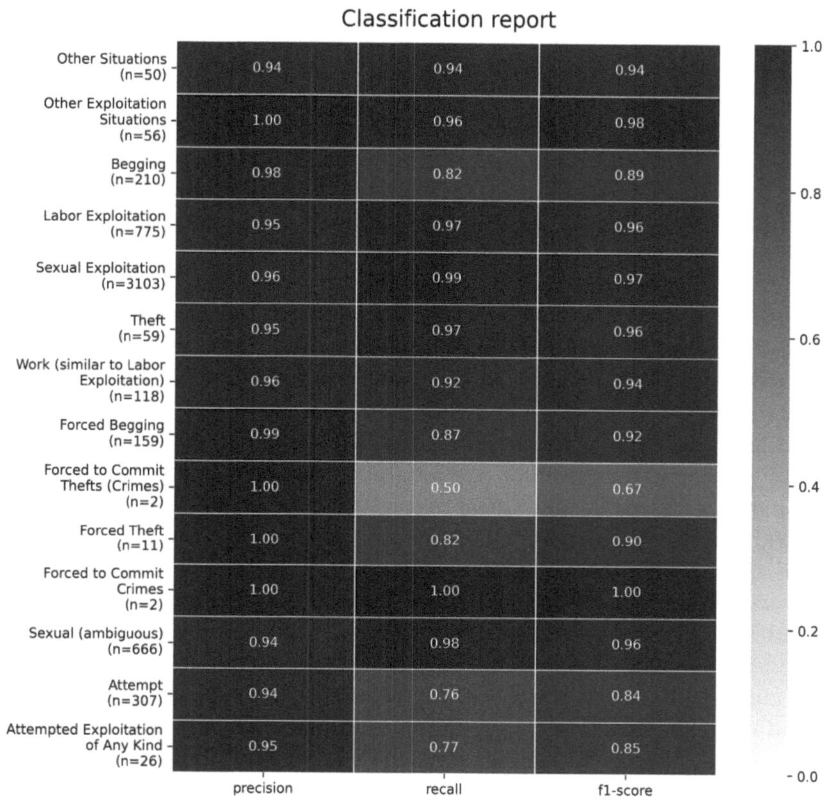

Fig. 2. Precision, Recall, and F1-Scores across Exploitation Categories

The MNIR (Multi-factorial Numerical Indicator of Risk) score is derived from contextual and socio-demographic factors, such as age, gender, education level, relationship with the recruiter, and environment of origin. Each factor contributes to a cumulative risk score ranging from 0 to 10. Scores between 0–2 indicate low risk, 3–5 represent moderate risk, 6–7 correspond to high risk, and 8–10 are classified as very high risk. By integrating this structured assessment with machine learning predictions, the system provides classifications that are both data-driven and aligned with practical risk evaluation frameworks used in the field.

Ultimately, however, the human factor remains decisive, particularly since these decisions concern matters as fundamental as the life and integrity of vulnerable individuals. This article emphasizes the role of AI as an instrument to enhance human judgment and improve the accuracy and timeliness of interventions, not as a replacement for human decision-making.

Looking ahead, future research may explore the integration of agentic AI systems capable of autonomously triggering predefined actions under controlled conditions—for example, automatically notifying a local social services team

DSS Recommendation

Exploitation type: Sexual Exploitation
AI probability: 84.33%
MNIR score: 6/10
Combined level: Very High
DSS recommendation: Urgent intervention: notify ANITP, specialized protection.

Fig. 3. Case-Level Decision Logic Combining Model Output and MNIR Indicators

when a case is classified as very high risk. Even so, the purpose of this study is not to delegate life-critical decisions to algorithms, but rather to strengthen the capacity of decision-makers to safeguard the fundamental values of life and human integrity.

By aligning machine predictions with MNIR social indicators and incorporating SHAP feature attribution for explainability, the DSS fulfills essential criteria of transparency, fairness, and traceability. These principles are consistent with ISO 31000 standards on risk management, which emphasize systematic evaluation, documentation, and communication of risks, as well as with the NIST AI Risk Management Framework (AI RMF), which requires explainable, accountable, and human-centered AI systems. Transparency is ensured through interpretable SHAP outputs, fairness by integrating socio-demographic risk factors to avoid exclusive reliance on statistical patterns, and traceability by storing predictions and contextual data in a structured database. Collectively, these features strengthen the DSS as a reliable decision-support tool for organizational and legal use.

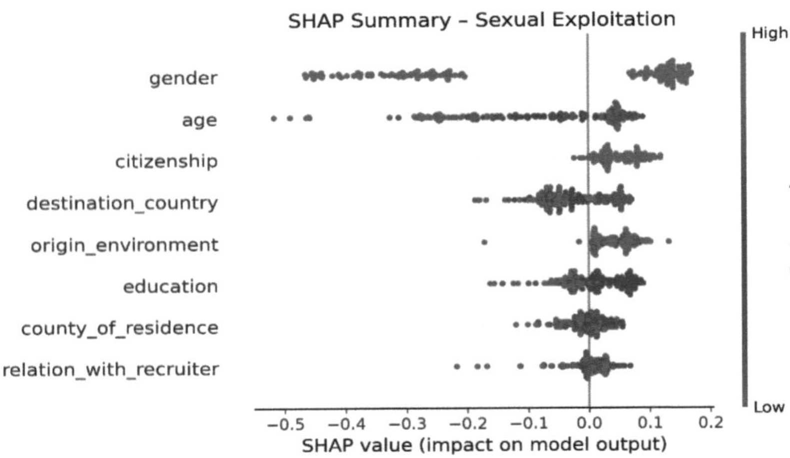

Fig. 4. SHAP summary plot illustrating the contribution of socio-demographic and contextual factors to model predictions

Figure 4 illustrates the SHAP summary plot for the Sexual Exploitation class, showing the relative influence of features on model predictions. Each point represents an individual case, with its position on the x-axis indicating whether the feature increased (positive values) or decreased (negative values) the probability of classification into this category. The color scale encodes the magnitude of feature values, where blue denotes lower values and red denotes higher values. This visualization aggregates results across multiple cases, highlighting which socio-demographic features most strongly influence the model's behavior.

The analysis indicates that gender, age, and destination country exert the greatest influence on classification outcomes, while education and recruiter relationship also contribute with more distributed effects. Such aggregate explainability is critical for ensuring interpretability and accountability, enabling decision-makers to understand the drivers of predictions rather than treating the model as a "black box". Furthermore, the DSS interface allows users to interactively select the exploitation class and the number of cases analyzed, thereby enhancing transparency and adaptability to diverse decision-making needs.

3.4 Prototype Development and Future Directions

Unlike large-scale international systems, the proposed DSS operates at the level of individual case triage. Polaris aggregates anonymized hotline data from across the United States to produce policy-level statistics for advocacy and awareness [35]. Frontex, through initiatives such as Operation Themis launched in 2018, coordinates transnational maritime patrols in the Central Mediterranean, focusing on securing EU external borders, disrupting smuggling networks, and conducting search-and-rescue missions [36,37]. Similarly, the International Organization for Migration (IOM) implements global counter-trafficking programmes that provide direct assistance and protection to victims in more than 100 countries worldwide [37]. By contrast, the DSS presented in this paper delivers case-level, explainable risk assessments aligned with Romanian legal standards. This distinction enables prompt, localized decision-making while ensuring transparency, traceability, and fairness through the integration of socio-demographic risk indicators (MNIR) and SHAP explainability.

Future development will prioritize integration with NGOs and law enforcement, as well as the deployment of referral alerts, mobile-ready dashboards, and real-time functionality. The harmonization of exploitation categories using natural language processing methods such as Word2Vec or BERT will improve consistency. Secure connectivity with external case management systems will be ensured through RESTful APIs. This scalability is supported by insights from Boss et al. [38], who highlight the importance of developing robust partnerships in supply chain contexts, a principle applicable to coordinating with external stakeholders in risk management systems.

In the long term, the DSS will evolve into a continuous learning system that adapts to new data and prevents model drift. It will expand into related areas such as domestic violence and child exploitation, thereby transforming into a broader risk assessment tool. Ethical AI provisions will remain central to this development, addressing issues of bias, data privacy, and human oversight, while maintaining compliance with ISO 31000 and the NIST AI RMF. This aligns with the strategic risk frameworks proposed by Iverson [39] and the decision-making technologies outlined by Frederic and Humphreys [40], which emphasize scalable and ethical system design.

4 Conclusions

This study introduces a decision support system (DSS) for assessing human trafficking risks, combining Random Forest classifiers with socio-demographic indicators from the Romanian National Identification and Referral Mechanism (MNIR), including age, gender, education, and recruiter relationship. The prototype generates case-level probability estimates for exploitation types, achieving a weighted F1-score of 0.96, while MNIR scores provide context-specific risk evaluations aligned with Romanian Law 678/2001 and European standards.

The system ensures traceability by storing predictions in a structured database, allowing practitioners to review and audit outcomes. It supports social workers, NGOs, and law enforcement by enabling earlier detection of high-risk cases (e.g., MNIR scores of 6–10) and guiding resource allocation, such as prioritizing counseling or investigations. The DSS enhances human decision-making by providing reliable, data-driven recommendations, while final decisions remain with professionals to uphold ethical responsibility.

Future improvements will address overlapping exploitation categories using natural language processing (e.g., Word2Vec or BERT), extend predictions to related areas like domestic violence and child exploitation, and integrate with institutional systems through secure APIs. These steps will align the DSS with ISO 31000 and NIST AI Risk Management Framework standards, ensuring scalability and ethical compliance.

This work shows how AI can assist human-centered risk management, offering transparent, interpretable, and auditable predictions to better protect vulnerable individuals.

AI Usage Declaration: AI-based tools were used only to rephrase and improve the clarity of some sentences. All intellectual content of this manuscript is solely the author's own.

References

1. Schroeck, M., Shockley, R., Smart, J., Romero-Morales, D., Tufano, P.: Analytics: the real-world use of big data. IBM Glob. Bus. Serv. **3**(4), 1–23 (2012)
2. Bardoscia, M., Battiston, S., Caccioli, F., Caldarelli, G.: Roads to financial network instability. Nat. Commun. **8**(1), 14416 (2017)
3. Schlegel, G.L., Trent, R.J.: Supply Chain Risk Management: An Emerging Discipline. CRC Press (2014)
4. Tohidi, H.: Role of risk management in IT systems of organizations. Procedia Comput. Sci. **3**, 881–887 (2011)

5. Suarez, D., et al.: Integrated decision support for disaster risk management: aiding preparedness and response decisions in wildfire management. Inf. Syst. Res. (2024)
6. Tan, P.-N., Steinbach, M., Karpatne, A., Kumar, V.: Introduction to Data Mining. Pearson (2019)
7. Brynjolfsson, E., McAfee, A.: The business of artificial intelligence. Harvard Bus. Rev. (2017)
8. Jordan, M.I., Mitchell, T.M.: Machine learning: trends, perspectives, and prospects. Science **349**(6245), 255–260 (2015). https://doi.org/10.1126/science.aaa8415
9. Agrawal, A., Gans, J., Goldfarb, A.: The Simple Economics of Artificial Intelligence. Harvard Business Review Press, Prediction Machines (2018)
10. Culp, C.L.: The Risk Management Process: Business Strategy and Tactics. John Wiley and Sons (2001)
11. Hardy, K.: Enterprise Risk Management: A Guide to Government Professionals. Jossey-Bass (2015)
12. Power, D.J.: Decision Support Systems: Managerial Concepts and Resources. Quorum Books (2002)
13. Zheng, T., et al.: Real-time intelligent big data processing. Sci. China Inf. Sci. **62**(8) (2019)
14. Hand, D.J., Henley, W.E.: Statistical classification methods in consumer credit scoring. J. Roy. Stat. Soc. Ser. A **160**(3), 523–541 (1997)
15. Bolton, R.J., Hand, D.J.: Statistical fraud detection: a review. Stat. Sci. **17**(3), 235–249 (2002)
16. Boucher, J.-P.: Bonus-malus scale models: creating artificial past claims history. Ann. Actuarial Sci. **17**(1), 36–62 (2023). https://doi.org/10.1017/S1748499522000100
17. Binns, R.: Fairness in machine learning: lessons from political philosophy. In: Proceedings of the 2018 Conference on Fairness, Accountability and Transparency, pp. 149–159 (2018)
18. He, H., et al.: Security aspects of cyber-physical systems which employ IoT. In: IEEE CEC, pp. 1015–1021 (2016)
19. Lundberg, S.M., Lee, S.-I.: A unified approach to interpreting model predictions. In: NeurIPS (31st Conference) (2017)
20. Ribeiro, M.T., Singh, S., Guestrin, C.: Why should I trust You?: Explaining the predictions of any classifier. In: Proceedings of the 22nd ACM SIGKDD International Conference on Knowledge Discovery and Data Mining (KDD 2016), pp. 1135–1144. ACM, New York, NY, USA (2016). https://doi.org/10.1145/2939672.2939778
21. Shim, J.P., Warkentin, M., J.F., Courtney, M., Power, D.J., Sharda, R., Carlsson, C.: Past, present, and future of decision support technology. Decis. Support Syst. **33**(2), 111–126 (2002)
22. Altman, E.I., Sabato, G.: The modelling of credit risk related to SMEs: the evidence of U.S. market. Abacus **43**(3), 332–357 (2007)
23. Turban, E., et al.: Decision Support, Business Intelligence Systems. Pearson (2010)
24. Brynjolfsson, E., McAfee, A.: Machine, Platform, Crowd. W. W. Norton & Company (2017)
25. Dean, J., Ghemawat, S.: MapReduce: simplified data processing on large clusters. Commun. ACM **51**(1), 107–113 (2008)
26. Doshi-Velez, F., BKim, F.: Towards a Rigorous Science of Interpretable Machine Learning. arXiv preprint (2017)

27. Gubbi, J., Buyya, R., Marusic, S., Palaniswami, M.: Internet of Things (IoT): a vision, architectural elements, and future directions. Future Gener. Comput. Syst. **29**(7), 1645–1660 (2013)
28. Batini, C., Scannapieco, M.: Data and Information Quality: Dimensions, Principles and Techniques. Springer (2016)
29. Lipton, Z.C.: The myths of interpretability of models. Commun. ACM **61**(10), 36–43 (2018)
30. Lazer, D., et al.: Big data analytics and Google flu. Science **343**(6176), 1203–1205 (2014)
31. Litan, R.E., Wallison, P.J.: Describing the place of big data on the financial regulatory reform. Technical report, American Enterprise Institute (2017)
32. Mittelstadt, B.D., Allo, P., Tadddeo, M., Wachter, S., Fioridi, L.: The ethics of algorithms: mapping the debate. Big Data Soc. **3**(2) (2016)
33. Kotter, J.P.: Leading Change. Harvard Business School Press (1996)
34. National Agency Against Trafficking in Persons (ANITP). Open data on human trafficking victims (2015–2024) (2023). https://anitp.nai.gov.ro/date-deschise/
35. Polaris Project: Analysis of 2021 Data from the U.S. National Human Trafficking Hotline (2021). https://polarisproject.org
36. European Border and Coast Guard Agency (Frontex): Frontex launching new operation in Central Med. Themis (2018). https://www.frontex.europa.eu/media-centre/news/news-release/frontex-launching-new-operation-in-central-med-yKqSc7
37. International Organization for Migration (IOM): Counter-Trafficking Programme (2023). https://www.iom.int/counter-trafficking
38. Modi, S.B., Mabert, V.A.: Supplier development: improving supplier performance through knowledge transfer. J. Oper. Manag. **25**(1), 42–64 (2007)
39. Iverson, D.: Strategic Risk Management. Wiley (2013)
40. Adam, F., Humphreys, P.: Encyclopedia of Decision Making and Decision Support Technologies (2008)

Author Index

K. Wącel (Ed.): BIS 2025 Workshops, LNBIP 568, p. 127, 2026.
https://doi.org/10.1007/978-3-032-11651-2

MIX
Papier aus verantwortungsvollen Quellen
Paper from responsible sources
FSC® C105338

If you have any concerns about our products,
you can contact us on
ProductSafety@springernature.com

In case Publisher is established outside the EU,
the EU authorized representative is:
Springer Nature Customer Service Center GmbH
Europaplatz 3, 69115 Heidelberg, Germany

Printed by Libri Plureos GmbH
in Hamburg, Germany